BALANCE WITHIN

A YOGIC AND SCIENTIFIC APPROACH TO WOMEN'S HORMONAL HEALTH

NIDHI KAGRANA

Clever Fox®
PUBLISHING
Chennai • Bangalore

CLEVER FOX PUBLISHING
Chennai, India

Published by CLEVER FOX PUBLISHING 2026

ISBN: 978-93-7500-624-4

ACKNOWLEDGEMENTS

No book is written in isolation. ***Balance Within*** is the result of many quiet conversations, unwavering support, and shared wisdom along the way.

My sincere thanks to Dr. Hansa Jairaj, Director of The Yoga Institute, Mumbai, for the foundational training that began this journey. I begin with deep gratitude to my Guru, Dr. Satyam Tripathi, Union Yoga Ayurveda, Singapore, under whose guidance I formally studied yoga therapy and was introduced to its holistic approach to wellbeing. His trust in me as a co-author of *Yoga for Spinal Issues and Alignment* planted the first seed of confidence that I could write a book of my own.

To my parents, my father-in-law, my late mother-in-law, and all family members - your blessings form the unseen foundation beneath every step I take. Your values, resilience, and faith have quietly guided this journey.

To my husband, **Samir**, thank you for your steady encouragement, endless patience, and for calmly listening to countless drafts, ideas, and last-minute edits. And to my daughters, **Tvesha and Nyasha**, who contributed everything from image edits to hormone debates at the dinner table - you have shown me that growth is truly a family project. This book carries your imprint in more ways than you realize.

To Shubha Joshi, my mentor, thank you for continually pushing me to evolve - not just outwardly, but inwardly - and for encouraging me to step more confidently into my voice.

I am grateful to my Balance2Bliss team and the team at Clever Fox Publishing for their support in bringing this work to life.

To my friends in Singapore, your support, encouragement, and belief in me have meant more than you know. Living away from home feels lighter because of the community we have built together. Thank you for always being there for me and cheering me on.

And finally, to the women I have had the privilege of working with over the years - this book is deeply shaped by you. Your stories, vulnerabilities, resilience, and honesty have taught me more than any textbook could. The questions you asked, the struggles you shared, and the courage you showed in understanding your own bodies helped me refine, rethink, and deepen my approach. This book carries your lived experiences within its pages.

INTRODUCTION

The Night I Began Listening

It was an ordinary evening.
My teenage daughters and I were sitting on the floor, huddled around a phone, playing a simple drawing game. One person would sketch on the screen, and the others had to guess. We were laughing, competing lightly, enjoying that rare moment.
I love those moments.

It was my turn to guess. The drawing was simple. My daughter had sketched something obvious. The other guessed it immediately. I looked at the phone. I knew the word. I just couldn't retrieve it. It sat somewhere in my mind, just out of reach. They laughed gently - not unkindly, just playfully.
"Mom, how could you not guess that?"

We moved to the next round. It happened again. Another simple word. Another blank pause. And then I felt it - a wave rising unexpectedly in my chest. Not anger. Not embarrassment. Something deeper.

Before I understood what was happening, tears filled my eyes. Not dramatic tears. Not a breakdown. Just a sudden emotional surge that felt unfamiliar. I remember telling myself quietly, *this is nothing. It's just a game. Why are you reacting like this?*
But the tears came anyway.

I am not someone who cries easily. I have always been emotionally steady. I have handled pressure, responsibility, and change throughout my life - calmly.
Yet in that small, ordinary moment, something felt different.
That night was not about a forgotten word.

It was a whisper.

Later, a corporate client in her early forties shared a similar moment with me.
She was presenting to senior leadership - confident, experienced, well-prepared. She suddenly forgot what she was about to say in the middle of the presentation. Her mind went blank for a few seconds. She recovered smoothly. No one noticed.
But afterward, she sat alone in her car and cried.
"I've always been sharp," she told me.
"I've always handled pressure. Why do I suddenly feel… fragile?"
Different life. Different setting. Same whisper.

After 35 - and often more noticeably in the early 40s - subtle hormonal shifts begin influencing the body in ways most women are never prepared for: sleep becomes lighter, stress feels stronger, recovery takes longer, emotions rise more quickly.
Memory feels less immediate.
These changes are rarely dramatic.
They are quiet. And because they are quiet, we dismiss them.
We call it stress.
We call it aging.
We call it weakness.

And often, we blame ourselves.

But nothing is wrong with you.
Your body is not failing. It is transitioning.

Hormones are deeply connected to rhythm - sleep cycles, breath patterns, nervous system balance, nourishment, light exposure, and emotional regulation. Modern life disrupts those rhythms constantly. What we interpret as "losing control" is often simply a body asking for a different kind of support.

I wrote this book not as a medical diagnosis, and not as a motivational message.
I wrote it as a woman who lived this shift.

As someone who practiced yoga since childhood and later trained deeply in yoga therapy, I believed effort was the answer-until my own body taught me otherwise. The solution was not pushing harder. It was learning to regulate differently: through movement that restores instead of depletes, through breath that steadies instead of stimulates, and through nourishment that stabilizes rather than spikes.

This book is for the woman who:
Appears strong on the outside,
Feels slightly unsettled within,
Manages everything,
But rarely pauses for herself.

Whether you lead in a boardroom or hold your family together at home, if you have felt these subtle shifts and quietly wondered, *"What is happening to me?"* you are not alone. And you are not late.

That evening on the floor with my daughters was not the moment I broke.

It was the moment I began listening.

And this book is an invitation for you to do the same.

Thank you for reading,

Nidhi

CONTENTS

PART 1

THE SHIFT AFTER 35

CHAPTER 1

WHEN YOUR BODY BEGINS TO WHISPER

The quiet changes every woman feels—but rarely talks about.

I remember the first time my body surprised me.

It was an ordinary morning in Singapore warm and familiar and I was moving through a Surya Namaskar I had practiced since childhood. The sequence was the same. The breath was steady. And yet, something felt different.

Not pain.
Not illness.
Just a quiet sense that my body was no longer responding the way it once had.

My joints needed more time to warm up.
My breath felt shorter, less forgiving.
And later that night, I woke up at 3 a.m.—wide awake, my mind alert for no obvious reason. It wasn't the first time. It had been happening for weeks.

At first, I did what most women do. I dismissed it.

Stress, I told myself.
Work.
Too much on my plate.

After all, I was healthy and active. There was no reason to question my body.

But the whispers continued.

Subtle, almost easy to ignore:

- sleep that became unpredictable
- emotions that felt closer to the surface
- energy that dipped without explanation
- a body that no longer responded to "pushing through."

I was in my late 30s when I realized something important:
My body wasn't failing me. It was asking me to listen.

What many women don't realize and what I didn't understand then—is that hormonal changes don't begin suddenly or dramatically. They unfold quietly, often years before we have words for them.

Before diagnosis.
Before labels.
Before menopause is ever mentioned.

Only later did I understand that these early shifts are part of a much longer hormonal transition—a natural process that every woman undergoes in her own time.

The problem is not the change.

The problem is that women are rarely taught how to recognize it.
We are taught to be resilient.
To adapt.
To keep going.

So, when our bodies begin to speak differently, we assume we are doing something wrong.

We blame ourselves for feeling tired.
For being more emotional.
For not recovering as quickly.
We need more rest than we used to.

In my work with women over the years, I've heard the same questions whispered again and again:
"Is this normal?"
"Why do I feel so different?"
"Am I just not coping as well as before?"

Here is what I want you to know—clearly and gently:

You are not imagining this.
You are not weak.
And you are not alone.

These whispers are not problems to be fixed.
They are messages—signals that your body is entering a new phase and asking for a different kind of care.

When we respond early, with awareness instead of resistance, this phase can become deeply grounding rather than disruptive.

This book is not about fighting your body or forcing balance.
It is about understanding what is changing and learning how to support yourself with wisdom, compassion, and the right tools.

If you are here because something in you feels different, trust that instinct.

Your body is not betraying you.
It is guiding you.

And in the next chapter, we will begin by understanding what is changing inside you—so you can respond with clarity, not confusion.

CHAPTER 2

THE HORMONE MAP WITHIN YOU

Understanding the chemistry that shapes your mood, weight, and energy.

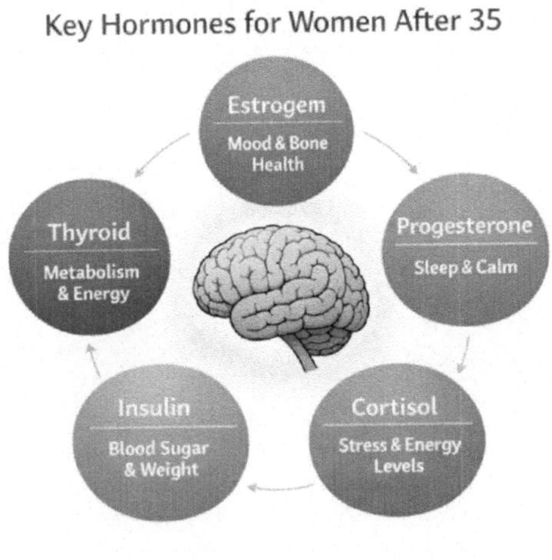

Figure 1: Key Hormones Influencing Women's Health after 35

If Chapter 1 was about listening, this chapter is about **understanding**.

Hormones are often spoken about as if they are mysterious, unpredictable forces—something that suddenly "goes wrong" in women's bodies. But hormones are not the enemy. They are messengers. They respond constantly to how we live, move, eat, rest, and cope.

When women tell me, "I feel out of balance," what they are often experiencing is not a single hormone problem—but a conversation between many hormones that has become strained.

Let's make this conversation simpler.

You don't need to memorize hormone names or numbers.

You just need a basic map.

2.1 Your Hormones: A Living Network

Hormones don't work in isolation. They function like a finely tuned orchestra. When one section plays too loudly or too softly, the entire performance changes.

After 35, this orchestra begins to shift its rhythm.
Some hormones become more sensitive to stress.
Some fluctuate instead of staying steady.
Some decline gradually, others erratically.

Understanding this network helps you respond with intelligence instead of frustration.

2.2 The Key Hormones Every Woman Over 35 Should Know

2.2.1 Estrogen – The Regulator

Estrogen influences far more than your menstrual cycle. It affects:

- mood and emotional resilience
- metabolism and fat distribution
- joint health
- skin and hair
- brain function

After 35, estrogen doesn't simply decrease. It fluctuates. These ups and downs often explain why symptoms feel inconsistent—fine one month, difficult the next.

2.2.2 Progesterone – The Calmer

Progesterone is often the first hormone to decline quietly.

It supports:

- deep, restful sleep
- emotional steadiness
- a sense of calm in the nervous system

When progesterone drops, women may notice:

- waking up between 2–4 a.m.
- increased anxiety or restlessness
- feeling "wired but tired."

This is not a personal failure. It is physiology.

2.2.3 Cortisol – The Stress Responder

Cortisol helps us cope with challenges. But chronic stress keeps it elevated for too long.

High cortisol can:

- disrupt sleep
- increase abdominal fat
- worsen anxiety
- interfere with estrogen and progesterone

For women balancing work, family, and emotional responsibilities, cortisol often becomes the loudest voice in the hormonal conversation.

2.2.4 Insulin – The Energy Manager

Insulin regulates blood sugar and energy use.

As hormones shift:

- insulin sensitivity may decrease
- weight gain becomes easier
- Energy crashes become more common

This is why women often say, "What used to work for my body doesn't work anymore."

They're right.

2.2.5 Thyroid Hormones – The Metabolism Regulators

The thyroid influences:

- energy levels
- metabolism

- temperature regulation
- mental clarity

Stress and hormonal shifts can affect thyroid function even when test results appear "normal."

2.3 Why Symptoms Rarely Come Alone

Sleep issues, weight gain, mood swings, fatigue—these are not isolated problems. They are connected signals.

For example:

- Poor sleep increases cortisol
- High cortisol affects insulin
- Insulin imbalance impacts estrogen
- Estrogen fluctuations affect mood and sleep

This is why quick fixes rarely work.
The body doesn't need control.
It needs coordination.

2.4 Why Awareness Changes Everything

Once you understand this hormonal map, two powerful things happen:

1. **You stop blaming yourself**
2. **You stop forcing your body to behave as it did at 25**

This is where many women feel relief for the first time.
Hormonal changes after 35 are not a decline.
They are a shift in needs.

And when those needs are met with the right movement, breath, food, and rest the body responds remarkably well.

In the next chapter, we will look at what happens when these signals are ignored and why so many women push through discomfort until their bodies are forced to speak louder.

CHAPTER 3

THE PRICE OF BEING "STRONG" ALL THE TIME

How pushing through quietly disrupts your health and how to stop.

Figure 2: The Hidden Cost of Constant Strength

She sat across from me at the end of a class, still in her work clothes, shoulders tense even as she tried to relax.

"I don't understand," she said. "I'm not sick. My reports are normal. But I feel exhausted all the time."

She was 42. A senior professional. Highly capable. Used to long hours and high responsibility. She told me she hadn't taken a proper break in years—not because she didn't want one, but because *she didn't know how to slow down without feeling guilty.*

Sleep came in fragments. Mornings began with coffee. Exercise felt harder than it used to, yet she pushed through because she believed discipline was the answer.

"What else can I do?" she asked.

"I can't afford to be weak."

That sentence stayed with me.

Because it's one I hear often—spoken quietly, almost apologetically by women who have learned to survive by being strong.

Most women don't think of themselves as neglecting their health.

They think of themselves as capable.

- Capable of handling long days
- Capable of managing work, family, and responsibilities
- Capable of pushing through fatigue, emotions, discomfort—because that's what life requires

Strength becomes a badge of honor.

And slowly, without realizing it, many women begin to live in a constant state of effort.

3.1 The Culture of "Push Through."

Somewhere along the way, many of us learned that rest must be earned.
That slowing down means falling behind.
That asking for support is a weakness.

So, when the body whispers through poor sleep, low energy, irritability, or anxiety, we respond by doing more.

More work.
More exercise.
More coffee.
More discipline.

What we rarely consider is this:

The body does not interpret constant effort as strength.

It interprets it as stress.

3.2 When Strength Becomes Strain

Physiologically, pushing through looks like this:

- cortisol remains elevated
- the nervous system stays in "alert" mode
- recovery becomes incomplete
- sleep becomes lighter
- digestion weakens

- hormones struggle to communicate clearly

Emotionally, it shows up as:

- impatience
- numbness
- emotional reactivity
- loss of joy
- a quiet sense of disconnection

Many women tell me,
"I'm doing everything right—yet I feel worse."

They are not wrong.

They are exhausted from being strong in a way the body was never designed for.

3.3 Why Willpower Stops Working After 35

In our twenties and early thirties, the body often tolerates imbalance.
Hormonal reserves are higher. Recovery is faster.

After 35, the same strategies begin to fail—not because we are weaker, but because the body requires a different approach.

What worked before—late nights, intense workouts, constant productivity—now creates backlash.

This is often when women feel betrayed by their own bodies.
But the truth is simpler and kinder:
The body is asking for cooperation, not control.

3.4 The Invisible Cost of Constant Stimulation

Modern life trains us to seek quick relief:

- constant scrolling
- quick rewards
- instant productivity
- constant distraction

These habits overstimulate the nervous system and create brief spikes of motivation or pleasure—followed by deeper fatigue.

Over time, the body begins to crave stimulation just to feel "normal."

This is not laziness.
It is neurological exhaustion.

And it quietly affects mood, hormones, sleep, and motivation.

3.5 Why Rest Alone Is Not Enough

Many women try to fix this by resting more:

- sleeping in on weekends
- taking short breaks
- escaping on holidays

While rest helps, it does not undo the underlying pattern.

The issue is not lack of rest alone.
It is **living in constant mental and emotional effort**.

The body needs rhythm.
Consistency.

Gentle regulation.

Not collapse after burnout.

3.6 A Different Definition of Strength

True strength after 35 looks different.

It looks like:

- choosing steadiness over intensity
- listening instead of overriding
- building habits, you can sustain
- allowing recovery to be part of progress

This is not about doing less.
It is about doing *what supports you*—repeatedly, patiently.

Many women fear that if they stop pushing, everything will fall apart.

What actually happens is the opposite:

When effort becomes wiser, the body begins to respond.

Sleep improves.
Mood steadies.
Energy returns gradually.
Motivation feels quieter but more reliable.

3.7 The Shift That Changes Everything

This chapter is not asking you to give up ambition or responsibility.

It is asking you to reconsider how you meet them.

The body does not thrive on force.
It thrives on consistency, safety, and rhythm.

When strength is paired with gentleness, the nervous system relaxes.
When effort is paired with awareness, hormones cooperate.

And this is where true balance begins.

In the next chapter, we will explore how modern stress quietly reshapes your hormonal landscape and why understanding this connection is essential before any healing can occur.

PART 2

HOW MODERN LIFE DISRUPTS HORMONES

CHAPTER 4

THE STRESS SPIRAL

What a modern life quietly reshapes your hormones.

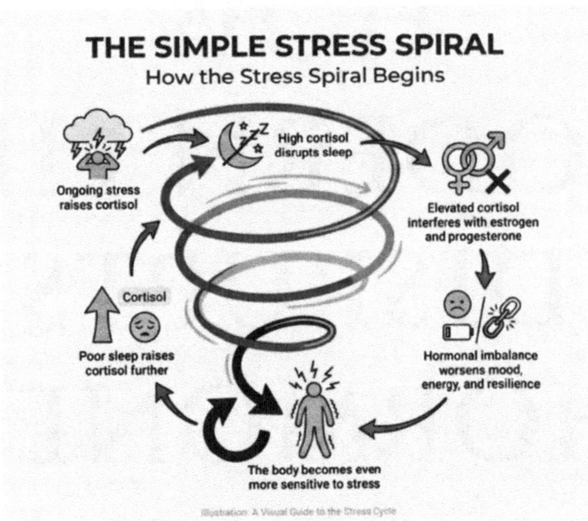

Figure 3: The Stress Spiral

She told me she was always tired—but never calm.

"I rest," she said. "I sleep when I can. I even take short breaks. But inside, it feels like my body is always switched on."

She wasn't describing stress the way we usually imagine it.
There was no crisis. No major trauma. No obvious emergency.

Just a constant sense of urgency.
A mind that never fully slowed down.
A body that didn't know how to relax anymore.

This is the kind of stress most women live with today.

And it is one of the most powerful forces shaping hormonal health after 35.

Stress is often misunderstood.

We think of it as something temporary—deadlines, problems, difficult phases. Something that will pass once life settles down.

But for many women, stress is no longer an event.
It has become a *state*.

4.1 Stress Is Not Just Mental

Stress is not only about what you think.
It is about how your nervous system responds to daily life.

Long working hours.
Constant multitasking.
Emotional responsibility at home and at work.
Digital overload.
Always being "available."

Even when life looks manageable from the outside, the body may still experience it as pressure.

And the hormone most affected by this is **cortisol**.

4.2 Cortisol: Helpful, Until It Isn't

Cortisol is not a bad hormone.
It helps you wake up in the morning.
It gives you focus.
It supports you during challenges.

The problem begins when cortisol stays elevated for too long.

When stress becomes constant:

- Cortisol stops following a healthy daily rhythm
- The nervous system remains on high alert
- The body struggles to return to a relaxed state

Over time, this affects everything.

4.3 How the Stress Spiral Begins

Here is how the spiral usually looks:

- Ongoing stress raises cortisol
- High cortisol disrupts sleep
- Poor sleep raises cortisol further
- Elevated cortisol interferes with estrogen and progesterone
- Hormonal imbalance worsens mood, energy, and resilience
- The body becomes even more sensitive to stress

And so, the cycle continues.

This is why many women say:
"I'm tired, but I can't rest."
"I'm exhausted, but my mind won't switch off."

4.4 Why Stress Feels Different After 35

Earlier in life, the body often recovers quickly.
Hormonal reserves are stronger.
Sleep rebounds more easily.

After 35, recovery requires more intention.

When progesterone begins to decline and estrogen fluctuates, the nervous system becomes more sensitive. What once felt manageable now feels overwhelming.

This is not because you are less capable.

It is because your body is asking for a different way of meeting stress.

4.5 The Myth of 'I'll Relax Later.'

Many women tell themselves:
"I'll slow down once this phase is over."
"Things will calm down after this project."
"I just need to get through this year."

But the body doesn't understand "later."

It responds only to what happens *repeatedly*.

If the nervous system never experiences safety and steadiness, it forgets how to relax—even when there is time.

This is why occasional rest is often not enough.

4.6 Stress Is Not Just External

Emotional stress plays a powerful role, too:

- unexpressed emotions
- the pressure to cope silently
- feeling responsible for everyone else's well-being
- constantly putting your needs last

The body does not separate emotional load from physical stress. It responds to both in the same way.

4.7 Breaking the Spiral Begins with Awareness

The goal is not to eliminate stress.
That is neither realistic nor necessary.

The goal is to **change how your body experiences stress**.

When the nervous system feels supported:

- cortisol begins to regulate
- sleep improves
- hormones communicate more clearly
- energy stabilizes
- emotional resilience increases

This does not happen through force or discipline.

It happens through rhythm, repetition, and gentle regulation.

4.8 A Quiet Shift That Makes a Big Difference

Many women are surprised to learn that small, consistent changes have more impact than dramatic interventions.

Short moments of calm during the day.
Breathing that slows the nervous system.
Movement that soothes rather than exhausts.
Evening routines that signal safety.

These are not luxuries.
They are biological signals.

And when they are repeated daily, the body responds.

In the next chapter, we will look more closely at how modern lifestyle patterns—sleep, screens, movement, and daily habits—continue this stress cycle, often without us realizing it.

Understanding this is the first step toward changing it.

CHAPTER 5

THE LIFESTYLE TRAPS WE FALL INTO

What everyday habits quietly drain hormonal balance?

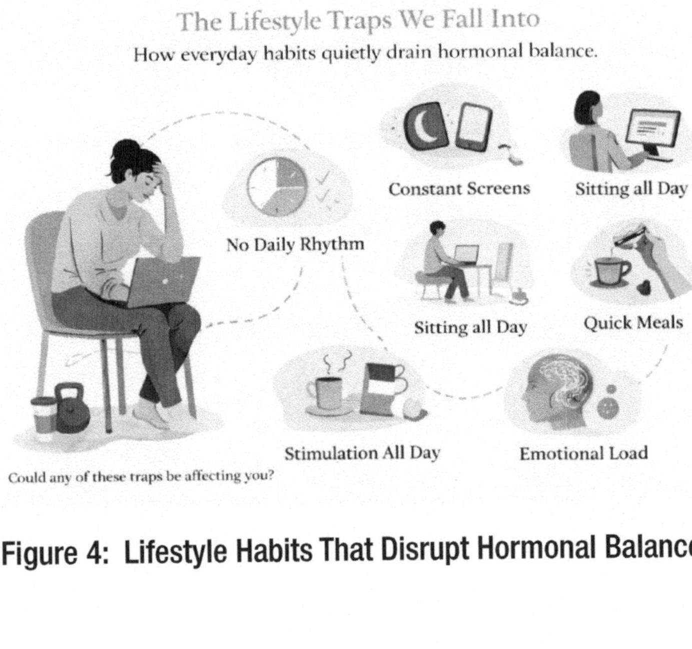

Figure 4: Lifestyle Habits That Disrupt Hormonal Balance

She told me she was "doing all the right things."

She woke up early. Managed work and home. Tried to eat well. Fit in exercise when possible. On the surface, her life looked balanced.

Yet her sleep was restless. Her energy dipped by the afternoon.
Her body felt heavy, uncooperative.
"What else can I change?" she asked.
"I'm already trying so hard."

What she didn't realize and what many women don't—is that hormonal imbalance rarely comes from one big mistake.

It comes from **small habits repeated daily**, often without awareness.

This chapter is about those habits.

5.1 The Problem Isn't What We Do Occasionally

Most women assume lifestyle problems come from:

- occasional late nights
- a stressful week
- a busy month

But the body is far less affected by what happens *sometimes* than by what happens **every day**.
Hormones respond to rhythm.
They listen to patterns.

And modern life quietly disrupts those patterns in ways that feel normal but are deeply taxing to the nervous system.

Trap 1: Living Without a Daily Rhythm

Irregular routines are one of the most overlooked stressors.

- waking at different times each day
- eating meals at inconsistent hours
- working late into the night
- sleeping and waking without a clear pattern

The body thrives on predictability.
When daily rhythms are missing, the nervous system stays alert—never fully settling.

This affects sleep, digestion, energy, and hormonal communication.

Trap 2: Constant Screen Exposure

Screens are everywhere—phones, laptops, tablets, televisions.
They keep us informed, connected, and productive.
But they also keep the mind stimulated long after the body needs rest.

- late-night scrolling
- checking messages before bed
- working on screens without breaks

Over time, this overstimulation interferes with the body's natural winding-down process, making deep rest harder to access.
Many women say:
"I go to bed tired, but my mind won't switch off."

This is not a lack of discipline.

It is a nervous system overload.

Trap 3: Sitting All Day, Then Forcing Exercise

Modern life encourages long hours of sitting at desks, in meetings, and in cars.

To compensate, many women push themselves through intense workouts, believing effort will “fix” what inactivity created.

But the body experiences this as:

- long periods of stagnation
- followed by sudden stress

After 35, this pattern can backfire—leading to fatigue, joint discomfort, and increased stress rather than vitality.

The body responds better to **regular, gentle movement throughout the day**, not extremes.

Trap 4: Eating on the Go, Thinking on the Go

Meals have become something we squeeze in between tasks.

- skipping breakfast
- eating hurriedly
- multitasking while eating
- irregular meal timing

Digestion begins in a calm state.
When meals are rushed or inconsistent, digestion weakens, energy fluctuates, and hormonal signals become less clear.

This often shows up as:

- bloating
- crazy cravings

- energy crashes
- unexplained weight gain

Again, this is not about food alone—it's about **how and when we eat.**

Trap 5: Depending on Stimulation to Get Through the Day

Coffee, sugar, constant activity—these are not indulgences.
They are survival tools for many women.

When energy dips, we stimulate.
When focus fades, we stimulate more.

Over time, the body begins to rely on external stimulation instead of internal balance.

This creates a cycle where rest feels uncomfortable, and stillness feels unfamiliar.

Trap 6: Ignoring Emotional Load

Lifestyle is not only physical.

Emotional habits matter too:

- constantly caring for others
- suppressing feelings
- avoiding difficult conversations
- never fully switching off emotionally

The body does not separate emotional stress from physical stress.

Both place demands on the same hormonal and nervous systems.

5.2 Why These Traps Feel Normal—but Aren't Neutral

None of these habits seems extreme.
Most are socially accepted—even encouraged.

But together, they create a body that is:

- always alert
- rarely fully rested
- constantly adapting
- slowly depleted

This is why many women feel tired even when life appears "manageable."

5.3 Awareness Is the First Shift

This chapter is not asking you to change everything at once.

It is asking you to **notice**.

Notice:

- where your days lack rhythm
- where stimulation replaces rest
- where effort replaces ease

Because awareness changes how the body responds.

When small habits shift—consistently, gently—the nervous system begins to soften.
And when the nervous system softens, hormones begin to cooperate.

In the next chapter, we will explore **why yoga works so effectively for hormonal health**—and how it offers a different approach from simply doing more.

PART 3

THE YOGIC ANSWER: MOVEMENT, BREATH & MIND

CHAPTER 6

WHY YOGA WORKS FOR HORMONES

Not as exercise—but as regulation.

Natania, 43 years old, an IT professional, told me she had tried yoga before.

"Honestly," she said, "it felt too slow. I thought I needed something more intense."

A few months later, she returned—not because she wanted flexibility, but because her sleep was broken, her anxiety unpredictable, and her body exhausted from trying to keep up.

This time, we didn't focus on poses.
We focused on **how her body felt before, during, and after movement**.

That changed everything.

6.1 Yoga Is Not About Doing More

Many women approach yoga the same way they approach everything else—with effort.
They push deeper.
They try to perform.
They compare.

But yoga was never meant to be another form of exertion.

Studies published by Harvard researchers found that programs incorporating yoga and meditation strengthened the relaxation response and lowered stress hormone activity.

At its core, yoga is a system of regulation of the body, the breath, and the mind.

And this is exactly why it works so effectively for hormonal health.

6.2 The Body Responds to Safety, Not Force

Hormones do not respond well to pressure.

They respond to:

- steadiness
- rhythm
- safety
- repetition

This is where yoga differs fundamentally from many modern fitness approaches.

Rather than overstimulating the nervous system, yoga:

- downshifts stress responses
- improves communication between systems
- restores balance gradually

When the nervous system feels safe, hormones cooperate.

6.3 Movement That Communicates, Not Competes

Yoga postures are not just stretches or strengthening exercises.

They are **messages** to the body.

- Gentle forward movements soothe
- Backward movements energise
- Twists regulate digestion and circulation
- Inversions support blood flow and endocrine communication

But the real power lies not in the posture—it lies in **how you move into it, breathe within it, and come out of it**.

This mindful movement tells the body:

"You don't need to stay on alert."

6.4 Breath: The Bridge Between Body and Hormones

Breathing is the fastest way to influence the nervous system.
In yoga, breath is not an accessory.

It is the guide.

Slow, steady breathing:

- calms cortisol
- supports emotional balance
- improves sleep quality
- enhances hormonal communication

This is why yoga therapy places such emphasis on **breath awareness**, long before advanced techniques are introduced.

Breathing teaches the body how to settle.

6.5 The Yogic View: Balance Comes from Consistency

Classical yoga reminds us that change happens through sustained, respectful practice over time—not intensity.

This wisdom is especially relevant after 35.
The body is no longer asking for extremes.
It is asking for continuity.
Gentle daily movement.
Regular breathing.
Mental steadiness.

This approach may feel subtle—but its effects are profound.

6.6 More Than the Physical Body

Yoga recognizes that the human experience is layered.

Physical symptoms are often connected to:

- emotional load
- mental overstimulation
- unresolved stress

By working with movement, breath, and awareness together, yoga addresses multiple layers at once—not in isolation.

This is why women often report improvements in:

- sleep
- mood
- digestion
- energy
- emotional resilience

Even before hormones, "balance" on paper.

6.7 Why Yoga Therapy Is Different

Yoga therapy does not ask:
"What can you push through?"

It asks:

- What does your body need today?
- What will support recovery, not depletion?
- How can movement feel nourishing rather than demanding?

This personalized, responsive approach is especially important during hormonal transitions.

There is no one-size-fits-all practice—only what supports your nervous system and rhythm.

6.8 A Different Relationship with Your Body

When practiced this way, yoga becomes more than a routine.

It becomes a conversation.
A way to listen rather than override.
A way to cooperate rather than control.

And this is where healing begins—not through effort, but through understanding.

In the next chapter, we will explore breathing more deeply and why it is one of the most powerful tools for restoring balance in a busy, overstimulated world.

CHAPTER 7

BREATH AS MEDICINE

Your most accessible tool for hormonal balance.

Figure 5: Breath as Medicine

A 39-year-old woman came to me. She was not asking about hormones.

She came because she couldn't sleep.

"I'm exhausted," she said, "but the moment I lie down, my mind won't stop."

Her days were full, her responsibilities endless, and her body permanently tense.

When I suggested starting with breath, she looked surprised. "Just breathing?" she asked. "I already breathe all day."

And that is where many women begin.

7.1 Why Breath Matters More Than We Realise

Breathing is automatic, but how we breathe changes constantly.

Under stress, the breath becomes:

- shallow
- fast
- irregular

Over time, this pattern signals the body to stay alert. Even when we rest, the nervous system does not fully settle.

This matters because breathing directly influences the **nervous system**, which in turn regulates the **stress response** and the hormonal systems connected to it.

Research in mind–body medicine shows that slow, controlled breathing can reduce stress activation and support nervous system balance. Institutions such as Harvard Medical School have highlighted breath-based practices as a key tool for calming the body's stress response and improving emotional regulation.

This is not spiritual theory.
It is physiology.

7.2 Breath and the Stress–Hormone Connection

Hormones do not function in isolation. They are regulated through constant communication between the brain, nervous system, and endocrine glands.

When breathing remains hurried or restricted:

- The nervous system stays in "fight or flight" mode
- Cortisol remains elevated
- Sleep becomes lighter
- Emotional reactivity increases

When breathing slows and becomes more rhythmic:

- The body shifts toward "rest and repair."
- Stress hormone activity begins to settle
- The mind becomes quieter
- Hormonal signaling improves

Breathing is the **fastest and most accessible way** to send a message of safety to the body.

For women after 35—when hormonal sensitivity to stress increases—this becomes especially important.

7.3 Breath in Yogic Wisdom

Long before modern science began studying stress physiology, yogic texts recognised the central role of breath in sustaining life and balance.

The *Praśna Upanishad* expresses this through a prayer to prāṇa, the vital life force:

Prāṇasyedam vaśe sarvaṁ
Tridivī yath pratiṣṭhitam |
Māteva putrān rakṣasva
Śrīśca prajñāśca vidhīyatām iti ||
(Praśna Upaniṣad 2.13)

This verse reminds us that **everything in the body functions under the influence of prāṇa**, and it compares prāṇa to a mother—protective, sustaining, and life-giving—asking that it guard us and bless us with vitality and clarity.

In modern terms, we might say this differently:
Breath influences the systems that keep us alive, regulated, and resilient—particularly the nervous system and stress response, which in turn affect hormonal balance.

When breath is supported gently and consistently, the body's own intelligence begins to restore equilibrium.

7.4 Why Gentle Breathing Works Better Than Force

Many women assume that breathing practices must be intense to be effective.

In reality, research consistently shows that slow, rhythmic breathing has a stronger calming effect on the nervous system than forceful or aggressive techniques.

From a yogic perspective, breath is not meant to be controlled harshly.
It is meant to be guided with awareness.

This is especially relevant during hormonal transitions, when the body responds better to steadiness than stimulation.

Breath practices work not because they demand effort, but because they create conditions where the body can soften, recover, and regulate itself.

7.5 Breath as a Daily Foundation, not a Technique

One of the most important shifts is this:
Breathwork is not something you "do once in a while."
It is something you return to **daily**, in small, realistic ways.

Even a few minutes of conscious breathing:

- before sleep
- between tasks
- after emotional stress

can begin to retrain the nervous system.

Modern research supports this principle as well: small, repeated interventions have a greater long-term impact on stress physiology than occasional, intense efforts.

Yoga has said this for centuries.
Science is now confirming it.

7.6 What This Means for You

You do not need special equipment.
You do not need long sessions.
You do not need to change your entire routine overnight.

You need a practice that:

- fits into real life
- respects your energy
- supports your nervous system
- creates a sense of safety inside the body

Breath is often the safest place to begin.

In the next chapter, we will explore how **movement**, when approached with the same principles of steadiness and awareness, can support hormonal balance without exhausting the body.

CHAPTER 8

MOVEMENT THAT HEALS, NOT EXHAUSTS

Why consistency matters more than intensity after 35

Figure 6: Movement That Heals

Michelle, a 51-year-old lady, told me she felt guilty for slowing down.

"I used to be so active," she said. "Now even a long workout leaves me drained. I feel like I'm losing my strength."

What she was really losing was not strength.
She was losing her **recovery**.

This is a common experience for women after 35.
The body no longer responds well to extremes—long periods of inactivity followed by intense effort or pushing through fatigue in the name of discipline.

What it begins to ask for instead is something different:

regular, intelligent movement.

8.1 Why 'Doing More' Stops Working

Earlier in life, the body often tolerates imbalance.

- late nights
- intense workouts
- inconsistent routines

After 35, hormonal sensitivity to stress increases. Recovery takes longer, and excessive physical strain can quietly add to the body's stress load.

Research in exercise physiology and women's health shows that overtraining and under-recovery can:

- increase stress hormone activity
- disrupt sleep

- worsen fatigue
- increase joint discomfort
- affect mood and motivation

This does not mean movement is harmful.

It means **how we move matters.**

8.2 The Yogic Understanding of Practice

Yoga has never defined practice as intensity.

Patañjali offers a simple but profound definition of sustainable practice:

"Sa tu dīrgha kāla nairantarya satkārāsevito dṛḍhabhūmiḥ"
—Yoga Sūtra 1.14

This sūtra tells us that practice becomes firmly established when it is:

- done over a **long period of time**
- without **interruption**
- with **respect and care**

This principle is especially relevant to movement after 35.

The body responds not to occasional effort, but to **steady signals of support.**

8.3 Movement as Communication

From a yogic perspective, movement is not just mechanical.

Every movement communicates something to the body:

- urgency or ease

- safety or strain
- cooperation or control

Gentle, regular movement tells the nervous system:

"You are supported. You don't need to stay on alert."

This creates conditions where hormones can function more smoothly.

8.4 What Science Confirms Today

Modern research supports what yoga has long understood.

Studies show that **moderate, consistent physical activity**:

- improves insulin sensitivity
- supports metabolic health
- reduces stress hormone levels
- improves sleep quality
- supports joint and bone health

In contrast, highly intense or irregular exercise—especially without adequate recovery—can increase physical stress and worsen fatigue in hormonally sensitive phases.

For women after 35, **regularity matters more than intensity**.

8.5 What Healing Movement Looks Like

Healing movement does not mean "doing less forever."
It means doing what the body can **recover from consistently**.

This may include:

- daily walking
- mobility and joint care
- gentle strengthening
- yoga practiced with awareness
- fewer but more intentional sessions

The goal is not exhaustion.

The goal is **continuity**.

8.6 Letting Go of Comparison

One of the quiet stressors many women carry is comparison:

- to their younger selves
- to others
- to past performance

Yoga encourages a different relationship with movement—one rooted in **listening rather than judging**.

When movement becomes responsive rather than performative, the body often responds with:

- steadier energy
- reduced pain
- improved confidence
- a sense of trust

8.7 Building a Sustainable Rhythm

Movement becomes healing when it is:

- predictable
- repeatable

- respectful of energy levels

This is not a loss of discipline.
It is a refinement of it.

The discipline now lies in **showing up gently, again and again**.

And over time, the body recognises this consistency as safety.

8.8 What This Means for You

You do not need to push harder to regain balance.
You need to move in a way your body can trust.

Yoga reminds us and science confirms that lasting change comes not from force, but from **steady, respectful practice over time**.

In the next chapter, we will explore the **emotional body**—and how meditation, particularly chanting-based practices, can support mood, mental clarity, and emotional balance during hormonal transitions.

CHAPTER 9

MEDITATION FOR EMOTIONAL BALANCE

Meditation as support for mood, clarity, and inner balance

Figure 7: Meditation for Emotional Balance

Many women tell me something like this:
"I can handle the physical discomfort.

What's harder is the emotional unpredictability."

They describe feeling more sensitive, more reactive, or emotionally tired without knowing why. Small things feel overwhelming. Thoughts loop. Sleep is affected—not because the body is restless, but because the **mind doesn't settle**.

This is not a weakness.
It is the emotional body asking for support.

9.1 Understanding the Emotional Body After 35

The emotional body is not separate from the physical body.

Hormonal changes influence:

- mood stability
- emotional resilience
- sensitivity to stress
- how deeply we feel things

At the same time, chronic stress and mental overload affect emotional regulation, which then feeds back into the body.

This is why many women feel:

- anxious without a clear reason
- emotionally flat or disconnected
- irritable or easily overwhelmed
- mentally fatigued even after rest

Addressing the emotional body is not optional—it is **essential** for hormonal harmony.

9.2 Why the Mind Struggles to Settle

Modern life keeps the mind constantly engaged:

- Scrolling through social media late at night
- Checking emails and messages repeatedly
- Watching series or streaming content to "switch off."
- Mentally replaying conversations or worrying about tomorrow's tasks

Over time, the mind forgets how to rest.
Trying to "force" stillness often backfires.
The mind resists effort just as the body does.

Yoga recognised this long ago.

9.3 A Yogic Principle from Cyclic Meditation

In the practice of Cyclic Meditation, a teaching drawn from the *Mandukya Upanishad* offers profound guidance on how to work with the mind:

**"Laye sambodhyet chittam vikṣiptaṁ śamayet punaḥ |
Sakāśāyaṁ vijānīyāt samapraptaṁ na cālayet"**

This teaching tells us:

- When the mind becomes distracted, **gently bring it back**
- When the mind begins to settle, **do not disturb it again**

The mind is not meant to be controlled forcefully.
It is meant to be guided with patience.

This principle forms the foundation of effective meditation—especially during emotionally sensitive phases of life.

9.4 Why Meditation Matters for Hormonal Health

Research in psychology and mind–body medicine shows that regular meditation practices:

- reduce emotional reactivity
- improve stress regulation
- support mental clarity
- improve sleep quality

When emotional stress reduces, the nervous system stabilises. And when the nervous system stabilises, hormonal communication improves.

Meditation does not change hormones directly.
It changes the **internal environment** in which hormones function.

9.5 Chanting Meditation: A Gentle Entry Point

For many women, silent meditation feels difficult—especially when the mind is already busy.

This is where **chanting-based meditation** becomes especially helpful.

Chanting provides:

- a point of focus
- rhythmic breathing
- vibration that soothes the nervous system

Practices such as **Om meditation** or **Mind Sound Resonance Technique (MSRT)** offer structure without strain.

They allow the mind to settle naturally, without effort.

9.6 Why Chanting Works So Well

From a yogic perspective, sound helps anchor awareness.

From a scientific perspective, chanting:

- slows breathing
- reduces mental chatter
- supports relaxation responses
- improves emotional steadiness

This makes chanting meditation particularly effective for:

- anxiety
- mood swings
- mental fatigue
- emotional overwhelm

Especially after 35, when emotional sensitivity increases, these practices offer **support without pressure**.

9.7 Meditation as a Relationship, not a Task

Meditation is not something to "achieve."

It is a relationship with your inner state.
Some days, the mind settles easily.
Some days it doesn't.

Both are part of the process.

Yoga reminds us that consistency matters more than results.
Returning gently—again and again—is what creates change.

9.8 What This Means for You

You do not need long sessions.
You do not need perfect silence.
You do not need to "empty" your mind.

You need a practice that:

- feels supportive
- meets you where you are
- calms rather than challenges

Meditation, especially when combined with sound and breath, can become a quiet anchor—helping you navigate emotional changes with greater steadiness.

9.9 Completing the Yogic Foundation

With breath, movement, and meditation, yoga offers a complete framework:

- **Breath** supports regulation
- **Movement** supports vitality
- **Meditation** supports emotional balance

Together, they form the yogic foundation for hormonal harmony.

In the next section of this book, we will shift toward **practical integration**—how food, lifestyle, daily rhythm, and support systems help sustain the balance you begin to build here.

PART 4

FOOD & LIFESTYLE FOR HORMONAL BALANCE

CHAPTER 10

EAT FOR BALANCE, NOT PERFECTION

The Foods That Nourish a Woman's Hormones and the Ones That Don't

Figure 8: A Balanced Plate for Midlife Health

Let me tell you about Ms. Chen.

She came to me at 45, frustrated and exhausted. "I'm doing everything right," she said, pulling out her phone to show me her calorie tracking app. "I eat 1,200 calories a day. I do spin class five times a week. I've cut out carbs. I meal prep every Sunday. But I keep gaining weight, I'm always tired, and I feel like I'm fighting my body every single day."

I looked at her food log. Breakfast: black coffee and toast. Lunch: salad with grilled chicken, no dressing. Dinner: steamed vegetables and fish. Snacks: rice cakes.

"Where's your healthy fat?" I asked. "And this isn't nearly enough protein for what your body needs right now."

She looked at me like, "But… I thought eating less was the answer. Low-calorie, low-fat, low-carb. That's what's always worked before."

Here's what I told her—and what I'm telling you:

What worked for your body at 25 or 30 doesn't work anymore. Your hormonal landscape has changed. Your metabolism has shifted. Your nutritional needs are different.

And the "diet culture" advice you've been following? It's not just ineffective now—it's actively working against you.

Three months later, Chen came back to see me. She'd increased her calories to 1,800. Added healthy fats. Doubled her protein. Included complex carbohydrates. Reduced her intense workouts to three times a week and added walking and yoga.

"I've lost the weight that wouldn't budge," she told me, "But more importantly, I have energy again. I'm sleeping. The brain fog is almost gone. I feel like I'm working *with* my body instead of against it."

This is what eating for hormonal balance looks like.

Not perfection.

Not restriction.

Not punishment.

Nourishment. Support. Balance.

10.1 Why Everything Changes After 35

Before we dive into what to eat, you need to understand *why* your nutritional needs have shifted.

During perimenopause and beyond, several major changes happen in your body:

Your metabolism slows down. Declining estrogen and progesterone affect how your body processes and stores energy. The metabolic rate that maintained your weight at 30 doesn't work the same way at 40.

Your insulin sensitivity decreases. Your cells become more resistant to insulin, making blood sugar regulation more challenging. This affects everything: your energy, your weight, your mood, your inflammation levels.

Your muscle mass naturally decreases. Without intervention, women lose 3-8% of muscle mass per decade after 30. Less muscle means slower metabolism and weaker bones.

Your body's inflammatory response increases. Fluctuating hormones can trigger inflammatory responses throughout your body, affecting everything from joint pain to hot flashes to brain fog.

Your stress hormones behave differently. Cortisol (your stress hormone) has always been there, but when estrogen drops, cortisol's effects become more pronounced, affecting your weight, sleep, and mood.

Your nutrient needs increase while absorption decreases. You need more of certain vitamins and minerals, but your body absorbs them less efficiently than it used to.

All of this means: food is no longer just fuel. It's information for your hormones. It's support for your transition. It's medicine.

And the good news? You have more control than you think.

10.2 The Anti-Inflammatory Foundation

If I could give you just one nutritional principle to focus on during this transition, it would be this: reduce inflammation.

Inflammation isn't just about joint pain or swelling. Chronic, low-grade inflammation in your body amplifies every single perimenopausal symptom:

- Makes hot flashes more frequent and intense
- Disrupts sleep quality

- Contributes to brain fog and memory issues
- Worsens mood swings and anxiety
- Accelerates weight gain, especially around the middle
- Increases risk of chronic diseases
- Affects skin, hair, and aging

Why does inflammation increase during perimenopause?

Estrogen has anti-inflammatory properties. As it declines, your body's natural inflammation control system weakens. Add to that the stress of this transition, poor sleep, and the standard modern diet—and you have a perfect storm for chronic inflammation.

So, what does anti-inflammatory eating actually look like?

It's simpler than you think. It's not about exotic superfoods or expensive supplements or complicated meal plans.

Focus on these foundations:

10.2.1. Colorful vegetables and fruits

Aim for at least 5-7 servings daily, focusing on:

- Leafy greens (spinach, kale, chard, lettuce)
- Cruciferous vegetables (broccoli, cauliflower, Brussels sprouts, cabbage)
- Colorful vegetables (bell peppers, tomatoes, beets, carrots, sweet potatoes)
- Berries (blueberries, strawberries, raspberries)
- Other fruits (apples, oranges, pomegranates)

The deeper and more varied the colors, the more anti-inflammatory compounds you're getting.

10.2.2. Healthy fats (yes, fat!)

This is where many women go wrong. Fat is not your enemy—it's essential for hormone production and reducing inflammation.

Include **healthy fats in moderation** as part of your daily meals:

- Olive oil (extra virgin, for cooking and dressing)
- Avocados
- Nuts (walnuts, almonds, cashews)
- Seeds (flax seeds, chia seeds, pumpkin seeds)
- Fatty fish (salmon, mackerel, sardines, herring)
- Ghee

10.2.3. Omega-3 fatty acids

These are particularly powerful anti-inflammatory agents. Aim for:

- Fatty fish 2-3 times per week
- Ground flaxseeds or chia seeds daily (1-2 tablespoons)
- Walnuts as snacks

10.2.4. Whole grains over refined carbohydrates

Replace white rice, white bread, and refined pasta with:

- Brown rice, quinoa, barley, oats
- Whole-grain bread and pasta
- Sweet potatoes

These provide fiber, vitamins, and minerals without spiking blood sugar.

10.2.5. Herbs and spices

Add liberally:

- Turmeric (with black pepper to enhance absorption)
- Ginger
- Garlic
- Cinnamon
- Rosemary, oregano, basil

These aren't just flavor—they're powerful anti-inflammatory agents.

What to minimize:

- Processed foods and packaged snacks
- Refined sugars and artificial sweeteners
- Trans fats and excessive saturated fats
- Excessive red meat
- Fried foods

Notice I said *minimize*, not eliminate. This isn't about perfection or deprivation. It's about shifting your overall pattern.

The goal is progress, not perfection. The goal is an overall pattern that supports your body, not a rigid set of rules that stresses you out.

10.3 Phytoestrogens: Nature's Hormone Support

Here's something fascinating: certain plants contain compounds that can act like very mild estrogens in your body.

These are called phytoestrogens—plant-based compounds that can bind to estrogen receptors and provide gentle hormonal support during perimenopause when your own estrogen is fluctuating.

The science behind this:

Phytoestrogens are much weaker than your body's natural estrogen—about 1/1000th the strength. But when your own estrogen is dropping, these plant compounds can help fill some of the gap, potentially easing symptoms like hot flashes, night sweats, and vaginal dryness.

Research shows that women in Asian countries, where phytoestrogen-rich foods are consumed daily, report significantly fewer menopausal symptoms than women in Western countries.

The best sources of phytoestrogens:

10.3.1 Soy products (the most researched)

- Organic tofu
- Tempeh
- Edamame
- Soy milk (unsweetened)

Important: Choose organic, minimally processed soy. Avoid heavily processed soy protein isolates in processed foods.

10.3.2 Flax seeds

- Ground flax seeds (your body can't digest whole seeds properly)
- 1-2 tablespoons daily in smoothies, yogurt, or oatmeal

10.3.3 Sesame seeds

- Tahini
- Whole or ground sesame seeds

10.3.4 Legumes

- Lentils
- Chickpeas
- Black beans, kidney beans

10.3.5 Whole grains

- Oats
- Barley
- Brown rice

A note about soy:

There's been controversy about soy and breast cancer risk. Current research shows that moderate consumption of whole soy foods (not processed soy isolates) is safe and may even be protective. If you have a history of hormone-sensitive cancers, discuss with your healthcare provider.

10.4 Protein: The Most Underrated Nutrient for Women

This is where I see women make the biggest mistake.

Most women I work with are eating nowhere near enough protein. And this deficiency is sabotaging everything—their muscle mass, their metabolism, their satiety, their mood stability, their blood sugar regulation.

Why protein matters more now:

10.4.1 Muscle preservation

After 35, you're fighting against natural muscle loss. Protein is the building block of muscle. Without adequate protein, you can't maintain—let alone build—the muscle mass that keeps your metabolism strong and your bones healthy.

10.4.2 Metabolic support

Protein has a higher thermic effect than carbohydrates or fats—meaning your body burns more calories digesting it. It also helps stabilize blood sugar, preventing the crashes that trigger cravings and energy dips.

10.4.3 Satiety

Protein keeps you full longer, reducing the constant hunger and snacking that many women experience during perimenopause.

10.4.4 Hormone production

Your body needs amino acids (from protein) to produce hormones and neurotransmitters that regulate mood, sleep, and stress response.

How much do you actually need?

According to the World Health Organization (WHO), healthy adults require approximately 0.8 grams of protein per kilogram of body weight per day to meet basic physiological needs. Emerging research in ageing and muscle health suggests that adults over 50 may benefit from a slightly higher intake — around 1.0–1.2 g/kg/day — to help preserve muscle mass, strength, and functional capacity with age. While 0.8 g/kg/day serves as a foundational guideline, women navigating midlife hormonal changes may often benefit from aiming slightly higher to support metabolic health, muscle preservation, and overall vitality.

Practically, this can look like having **2–3 servings of protein** across your meals each day — for example, a palm-sized portion of lean meat, fish, eggs, tofu, or daal, chickpeas, paneer at each main meal.

Common concerns:

"Won't that much protein damage my kidneys?" Not if you have healthy kidneys. This concern applies to people with existing kidney disease, not healthy individuals.

"I can't eat that much food!" You're not adding massive amounts—you're redistributing. Instead of a carb-heavy breakfast, add protein. Instead of a salad with minimal protein, add a substantial portion.

"I'm vegetarian/vegan—is this possible?" Absolutely. It requires more planning, but plant-based proteins combined throughout the day can easily meet your needs.

10.5 The Truth About Coffee, Sugar, and Wine

These are the three things women ask about most, and understandably so.
You don't need to give them up entirely. However, during hormonal transitions, **your tolerance often changes**, and awareness matters.

10.5.1 Coffee and Tea: Friend or Foe?

Coffee and tea are part of daily life for many women. In moderation, they are not inherently harmful. However, after 35, caffeine can have a stronger impact.

Caffeine may:

- trigger or worsen hot flashes and night sweats
- disrupt already fragile sleep
- increase anxiety and restlessness
- spike stress hormones
- interfere with calcium absorption (important for bone health)

What matters most is **individual response**. Some women tolerate caffeine well, while others notice new symptoms.

Practical guidance:

- Limit caffeine to **1–2 servings per day**
- Prefer consumption **before noon**
- Notice whether coffee or strong tea affects sleep, anxiety, or hot flashes
- Avoid using caffeine to compensate for poor sleep or fatigue

- If sleep issues persist, try a **2-week caffeine break** and observe changes

You don't need elimination, you need **attunement**.

10.5.2 Sugar: The Hidden Hormone Disruptor

Excess sugar is one of the most disruptive dietary factors during hormonal transitions.

High sugar intake can:

- destabilize blood sugar
- increase stress hormone release
- worsen insulin resistance
- increase inflammation
- intensify cravings, mood swings, and fatigue
- promote central weight gain

Added sugars are often hidden in foods marketed as "healthy," including:

- flavored yogurts
- sauces and dressings
- smoothies and juices
- granola, snack bars, and breads

Supportive approach:

- Read labels — ingredients ending in "-ose" are forms of sugar
- Aim to keep **added sugars low** while allowing natural sugars from whole fruits
- Pair sweets with protein or fat to slow blood sugar spikes

- Choose whole fruits over juices
- Apply the **80/20 principle**: consistency matters more than perfection

10.5.3 Wine and Alcohol: A Complicated Relationship

Alcohol often feels relaxing, but its effects during perimenopause are rarely neutral.

Alcohol can:

- disrupt sleep quality (even if it helps you fall asleep)
- worsen hot flashes and night sweats
- increase anxiety and low mood
- interfere with liver hormone metabolism
- destabilise blood sugar
- contribute to weight gain
- increase breast cancer risk
- impair gut health

Research consistently shows that even moderate alcohol intake carries increased risk for women, particularly during midlife.

A helpful experiment:

Consider going **alcohol-free for 30 days** and notice changes in:

- sleep quality
- hot flashes
- mood stability
- energy levels
- digestion

Then decide what level — if any — feels supportive.

If you choose to drink:

- Limit intake to **3–4 drinks per week**
- Choose lower-sugar options
- Avoid alcohol as a stress or sleep aid
- Stay hydrated and eat beforehand
- Observe how your body responds

The Takeaway

- You don't need rigid rules.

You need **awareness, moderation, and honesty about how your body responds now — not how it used to respond years ago**.

- Hormonal harmony is supported not by restriction, but by **informed choices made consistently**.

CHAPTER 11

THE LIFESTYLE UPGRADE

Dinacharya for modern women — rhythm over rigidity

Women don't struggle because they lack discipline.
They struggle because their days have lost rhythm.

Late nights followed by rushed mornings.
Long hours of sitting are broken by bursts of activity.
Screens until bedtime.
Irregular meals.
Constant mental stimulation with little recovery.

Over time, the body begins to feel unsettled. Sleep becomes lighter. Energy fluctuates. Mood feels less stable. Weight shifts despite best efforts.

This is not a failure of willpower.

It is a **lifestyle rhythm issue**.

11.1 Dinacharya: Daily Rhythm as Hormonal Support

In Ayurveda, this understanding of daily routine is called **Dinacharya**.

At its core, Dinacharya means:

Living in alignment with the body's natural cycles of activity, nourishment, and rest.
This is not about strict schedules or traditional rules.
It is about **predictable signals** that help the nervous system and hormones function smoothly.

Modern science supports this idea: regular routines reduce stress load, improve sleep quality, and support metabolic and hormonal regulation.

11.2 Key Lifestyle Anchors for Hormonal Harmony

Rather than changing everything at once, Dinacharya works best when you focus on a few **non-negotiable anchors** in your day.

11.2.1 Sleep Reset Routine

Sleep is not just rest — it is **hormonal repair time**.

Irregular sleep timing disrupts circadian rhythm, which affects cortisol, insulin sensitivity, and appetite regulation.

A supportive sleep routine includes:

- going to bed and waking up at roughly the same time
- reducing stimulation in the hour before sleep

- keeping evenings lighter and calmer

Harvard Health has highlighted that consistent sleep timing is as important as sleep duration for metabolic and hormonal health.

11.2.2 Sunlight and Circadian Rhythm

Morning light is one of the strongest signals for resetting the body clock.

Exposure to natural sunlight early in the day helps:

- regulate cortisol rhythm
- improve sleep quality at night
- support energy and mood stability

Even 10–15 minutes of daylight exposure soon after waking can make a difference.

This is Dinacharya in its simplest form — **aligning with nature's cues**.

11.2.3 Movement Habits (Not Random Exercises)

The body responds best to **regular movement**, not occasional extremes.

Daily movement supports:

- circulation
- joint health
- insulin sensitivity
- stress regulation

Movement doesn't need to be long or intense.
What matters is **consistency and timing**.

Gentle movement earlier in the day often supports energy better than late-night intense workouts, which can interfere with sleep.

11.2.4 Strength Training Essentials

After 35, maintaining muscle mass becomes increasingly important for:

- metabolic health
- blood sugar regulation
- bone strength
- long-term independence

Strength training does not mean heavy or aggressive workouts.

Simple, regular resistance - using body weight, bands, or light weights — a few times a week is enough to support hormonal health.

Consistency matters more than intensity.

11.2.5 Breath Breaks Throughout the Day

Stress often accumulates silently.

Short, conscious breathing pauses act as **reset points** for the nervous system.

Breath breaks:

- reduce stress response
- improve focus
- support emotional regulation

These don't require long sessions — even one or two minutes, repeated through the day, can help restore balance.

This is Dinacharya applied to the nervous system.

11.2.6 Digital Detox (Essential, Not Optional)

Constant screen exposure keeps the mind and nervous system overstimulated.

Excessive digital engagement:

- increases mental fatigue
- disrupts sleep
- elevates stress levels
- fragments attention

A digital detox doesn't mean abandoning technology.
It means **creating boundaries**, especially:

- in the evening
- during meals
- before sleep

Reducing digital input allows the body and mind to downshift naturally.

This has become one of the most important modern adaptations of Dinacharya.

11.3 Why Small, Repeated Changes Work

Harvard Business Review has consistently shown that small, repeatable habits are more sustainable and effective than drastic lifestyle overhauls — particularly for people managing high stress and multiple responsibilities.

Dinacharya works because it:

- reduces decision fatigue
- creates predictability
- builds trust within the body

Hormonal balance responds best to **steady signals**, not sudden change.

11.4 Lifestyle as Support, Not Control

Lifestyle practices are not about controlling the body.

They are about creating conditions where the body can regulate itself.

When daily rhythm improves:

- sleep deepens
- stress softens
- energy stabilises

- emotional resilience increases

Hormonal harmony is not forced.
It emerges when the body feels supported.

11.5 What This Means for You

You don't need:

- a perfect routine
- early mornings that don't suit you
- strict rules

You need:

- a few reliable anchors in your day
- consistency over intensity
- respect for your energy cycles

Dinacharya is not a checklist.
It is a **way of relating to time, energy, and self-care**.

PART 5

SUPPORT, FAMILY & SOCIETY

CHAPTER 12

YOU DON'T HAVE TO DO THIS ALONE

The power of support during hormonal transitions.

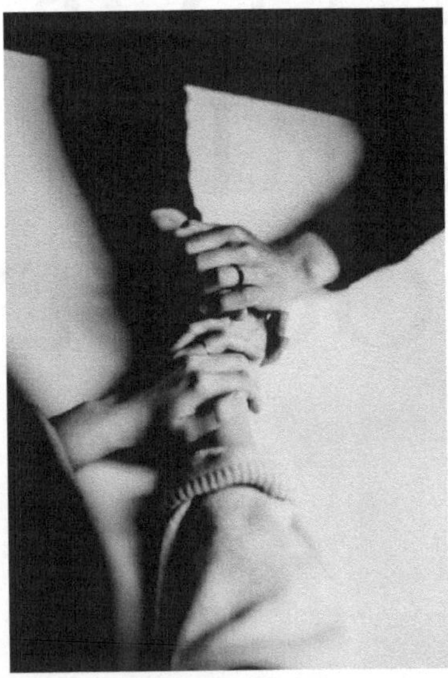

Figure 9: The Power of Support and Connection

There's a moment that happens in almost every yoga therapy session I conduct.

A woman sits across from me, listing her symptoms—the sleepless nights, the brain fog, the irritability, the exhaustion. Then she pauses, and almost always, she says the same thing:

"I feel so alone in this."

Sometimes she adds, "My husband doesn't understand. My family thinks I'm overreacting. My friends are too young to get it. I feel like I'm going crazy, and nobody sees it."

This isolation—this feeling that you're navigating this alone—is often more painful than the physical symptoms themselves.

And here's what breaks my heart: **you don't have to do this alone. But most women try to.**

12.1 The Invisible Labor of Transition

Let me paint a picture I see constantly:

You wake at 3 AM, drenched in sweat. You change your clothes, try to fall back asleep, and finally drift off at 5 AM—just before your alarm goes off. You drag yourself out of bed, exhausted.

You make breakfast for the family. Pack lunches. Get the kids ready. Answer work emails that came in overnight. Rush through your morning, running on fumes and coffee.

At work, you push through the brain fog, apologizing internally every time you forget a name or lose your train of thought. You sit through a meeting, feeling a hot flash rise, hoping nobody notices the sweat on your upper lip.

You come home to a partner who asks, "What's for dinner?" and kids who need help with homework. You manage everyone's needs, stuff down your irritability, and finally collapse into bed—only to wake again at 3 AM.

And through all of this, you haven't told anyone what you're going through.

Not really. Not fully. Maybe you've mentioned you're "not sleeping well" or "feeling stressed." But the full weight of it? The hormonal chaos, the physical discomfort, the emotional turbulence, the fear that this is your new normal?

You carry that alone.

12.2 Why We Hide

I've asked hundreds of women: "Why didn't you tell your family what you were experiencing?"

The answers are always similar:

"I didn't want to burden them." "They wouldn't understand anyway." "I'm supposed to be strong." "It feels like complaining." "I thought I should be able to handle it myself." "My mother never talked about this stuff." "I was embarrassed." "I didn't want to seem weak or old."

We've been conditioned to believe that our struggles—especially the ones related to our female bodies—are private matters we should manage quietly and efficiently, without disrupting anyone else's life.

But here's the truth: perimenopause and menopause are not individual experiences. They affect the entire household.

When you're not sleeping, it impacts your patience with your children. When you're exhausted, it affects your presence with your partner. When you're struggling with brain fog, it influences your ability to manage household tasks. When you're irritable, it changes the emotional atmosphere of your home.

This is not your failure. This is biology.

And pretending it's not happening—or trying to power through it invisibly—doesn't serve you OR your family.

12.3 What Support Actually Looks Like

True support at home doesn't mean your family takes over all your responsibilities or treats you like you're fragile. It means they *understand what you're going through* and adjust accordingly.

Support looks like:

Your partner says, "I know you're not sleeping well because of hormonal changes. What can I take off your plate so you can rest more?"

Your teenage daughter understands: "Mom's going through perimenopause, which means her hormones are changing. If she seems irritable, it's not about us—and she's doing her best."

Your family recognizes: "Mom needs 20 minutes alone after work to do her breathing practice. This helps her regulate her nervous system."

Your partner notices: "You seem overwhelmed. I'm handling dinner tonight."

Your family learning: "Hot flashes are real. If Mom suddenly opens all the windows in winter, we don't complain—we grab a sweater."

Support is not about being coddled. **It's about being seen, understood, and accommodated during a very real biological transition.**

12.4 The Conversation Most Women Avoid

I speak with women who've been married for 20 years, who've never had a real conversation with their partner about what's happening to their body.

"How do I even start?" they ask me.

Here's what I tell them: Start with education, not emotion.

When you're in the thick of symptoms—exhausted, irritable, overwhelmed—that's not the time to try to explain perimenopause to your family. They'll hear complaining. You'll feel dismissed. It becomes a conflict instead of a conversation.

Instead, choose a calm moment. Maybe after dinner, maybe on a weekend morning. And start with facts:

"I want to talk to you about something important that's happening to my body. I'm in perimenopause, which is the transition toward menopause. It can last 5-10 years and involves significant hormonal changes that affect sleep, mood, energy, and more. I want you to understand what's happening so we can navigate this together."

Then share specifics:

"These are some of the symptoms I'm experiencing: [list them]. These aren't things I can 'push through' or 'think positively' about. They're biological. And I need your support."

And be clear about what support means:

"Here's what would help me: [be specific]. More help with [task]. Understanding when I need alone time. Not taking it personally when I'm irritable. Asking 'what do you need?' instead of assuming."

The more you educate, the less they'll take it personally. The clearer you are about your needs, the better they can support you.

12.5 When Your Partner Doesn't Understand

I hear this often: "I tried to explain, but my husband just doesn't get it."

Sometimes this is because he's never been taught about perimenopause. Most men know about menopause vaguely—something about hot flashes when women are older—but they have no concept of the years-long transition, the hormonal chaos, the systemic effects.

Here's what can help:

12.5.1 Use analogies he can relate to

"You know how you feel when you haven't slept for two nights? That's my baseline right now because my hormones are disrupting my sleep."

"Remember when you threw your back out and couldn't move easily? That's what joint pain from hormone changes feels like—but it's not visible."

12.5.2 Share resources

Give him an article to read. Show him a video. Ask him to come to a doctor's appointment with you. Sometimes hearing it from a third party helps it click.

12.5.3 Be specific about the biology

"My estrogen and progesterone are fluctuating wildly. Estrogen affects serotonin in the brain—the same neurotransmitter that regulates mood. So, when I'm irritable or anxious, it's not about you. It's chemistry."

12.5.4 Request specific actions

Don't just say "I need support." Say: "I need you to handle bedtime with the kids on Tuesdays and Thursdays so I can do my yoga practice," or "I need you to take over grocery shopping for the next few months."

Men often want to help—they don't know how. Give them concrete tasks.

12.6 Include Your Children (Age-Appropriately)

How you talk to your children about what you're going through depends on their age, but I believe in age-appropriate honesty.

For younger children (under 10): "Mommy's body is changing, and sometimes that makes me feel tired or grumpy. It's not because of anything you did. I'm taking care of myself, and I love you very much."

For tweens and teens: "I want to talk to you about something called perimenopause. It's a natural transition that happens to women's bodies, usually starting in their late 30s or 40s. My hormones are changing, and that affects my sleep, my mood, and my energy. You might notice I'm more tired or irritable sometimes. I'm managing it, but I wanted you to know what's happening."

For teenage daughters especially: This is an opportunity to give them information you wish you'd had. Explain that this will happen to them someday, too. Normalize it. Remove the shame and secrecy around women's hormonal health.

"This is what women's bodies do. It's natural. And the more you know about it now, the better you'll be able to navigate it when your time comes."

You're not burdening them with this information. You're educating them.

12.7 The Ripple Effect of Speaking Up

Here's what I've witnessed repeatedly:

When a woman finally opens up to her family about what she's experiencing, something shifts. Not just for her, but for everyone.

Her partner becomes more attentive, more helpful, more patient—because he finally understands.

Her children learn that women's health matters, that hormonal changes are real and deserve respect.

Her teenagers (especially daughters) receive education about their own bodies and futures.

The whole family becomes more emotionally literate.

And the woman herself? She stops carrying the burden alone. She stops feeling crazy or broken. She realizes she's not failing—she's transitioning.

Silence keeps you isolated. Speaking up creates connection.

12.8 Building Your Home Support System

Here are practical ways to build support at home:

12.8.1. Schedule a family meeting.

Make this a formal conversation, not a side comment during a chaotic morning.

12.8.2 Create a symptom chart.

Put it somewhere visible (the fridge, your bathroom mirror). List your common symptoms. When family members see "Mom's having a low energy day" or "Hot flash alert," they know it's biology, not mood.

12.8.3 Establish non-negotiable self-care time.

"Every morning from 6:30-7:00 AM, I do my yoga and breathing practice. This is not optional—it's medicine. The house might be chaotic during this time, and that's okay."

12.8.4 Delegate specific tasks.

Sit down with your partner and divide responsibilities. What can permanently come off your plate? What can shift temporarily during particularly difficult phases?

12.8.5 Create a "bad day protocol."

When symptoms become severe, what's the plan? Maybe your partner automatically handles dinner. Maybe the kids know how to be more independent. Having a protocol removes the need to ask for help in the moment.

12.8.6 Check in regularly.

Once a week, ask your partner: "How are you feeling about everything? Do you need more information? Is there anything I need to tell you?"

Keep the conversation ongoing, not a one-time event.

12.9 When Home Support Isn't Possible

I know not every woman has a supportive partner or family. Some women are single parents. Some have partners who refuse to engage. Some live in households where their health concerns are minimized or dismissed.

If this is you, I want to say: **you still deserve support. You just need to build it elsewhere.**

This might mean:

- Finding a community of women going through the same thing (we'll talk about this in the next chapter)
- Working with a therapist who understands perimenopausal challenges
- Joining online support groups
- Leaning more heavily on friends
- Hiring help where possible—even just for a few hours a week

You cannot do this entirely alone. But your support doesn't have to come from within your home.

12.10 The Gift You're Giving

When you speak up about what you're experiencing—when you ask for support, when you educate your family, when you refuse to suffer silently—you're not just helping yourself.

You're changing the culture around women's health.

You're teaching your daughters that their bodies and their health matter. You're teaching your sons that women's experiences deserve respect and accommodation. You're teaching your partner that caregiving goes both ways. You're modelling that vulnerability is not weakness—it's honesty.

Every time a woman speaks up, it becomes a little easier for the next woman to do the same.

12.11 You Are Not a Burden

Let me say this clearly: **Your needs during this transition are not inconvenient. They are legitimate.**

You are not "too much." You are not "overreacting." You are not "making a big deal out of nothing."

You are going through a profound biological transformation, and you deserve support.

The right people—the people who truly love you—will want to understand and help. They might not get it perfectly right away. They might need education. They might make mistakes.

But they will try. And you deserve people who try.

You don't have to do this alone. You were never meant to.

CHAPTER 13

THRIVING AT WORK: HORMONAL HEALTH FOR CORPORATE WOMEN

How to stay productive without sacrificing your nervous system.

Figure 10: Workplace Stress and Hormonal Strain

The email arrived at 11:47 PM.

Sarah stared at her laptop screen, her eyes burning from exhaustion. She'd been up since 5:30 AM, powered through back-to-back meetings all day, skipped lunch (again), and was now trying to finish a presentation due tomorrow morning while her family slept upstairs.

She reached for her third cup of coffee of the evening—cold now and felt a familiar wave of heat rise through her chest. Another hot flash. The fifth one today.

Her brain felt foggy. She'd read the same paragraph three times and still couldn't absorb it. She'd forgotten two meeting times this week and had to apologize both times. Yesterday, she'd snapped at a junior colleague over something minor and felt terrible about it afterward.

Sarah is 47 years old. She's a senior director at a multinational corporation. She manages a team of 20 people across three countries. She's respected, accomplished, and by all external measures, successful.

She's also in perimenopause. And she's terrified that if anyone at work finds out what she's struggling with, everything she's worked for will crumble.

When Sarah finally came to see me, she broke down in tears. "I feel like I'm losing my edge," she said. "My memory isn't what it was. My focus comes and goes. Some days, I'm so exhausted I can barely think. But I can't slow down. I'm in a male-dominated industry. If I show any weakness, I'll be sidelined. Younger people are breathing down my neck. I have to perform—but my body won't cooperate."

This is the conversation happening in boardrooms, corner offices, and late-night work sessions across the world—except it's not happening out loud. It's happening in silence, in shame, in fear.

13.1 The Invisible Crisis in Corporate Environments

Here's what nobody talks about: Millions of highly accomplished women are navigating perimenopause and menopause while trying to maintain high-performance careers—and most are doing it completely alone.

The statistics are staggering:

- Women between 45-54 represent one of the fastest-growing segments in the workforce
- This is exactly the age when perimenopausal symptoms peak
- Up to 80% of working women experience menopausal symptoms
- Yet less than 30% feel comfortable discussing it at work
- Many women report that symptoms negatively impact their work performance
- Some consider leaving their careers entirely due to unmanaged symptoms

Think about that: women are reaching the peak of their professional expertise and leadership capability at the same time their bodies are going through a profound hormonal transition.

And instead of supporting them through it, most workplaces pretend it's not happening.

13.2 Why Corporate Culture Makes Everything Harder

Let me be clear about something: perimenopause is challenging regardless of your work situation. But corporate environments—especially high-pressure, competitive ones—create unique challenges:

13.2.1 The culture of invincibility

In many corporate settings, especially male-dominated industries, there's an unspoken expectation: you show up, you perform, you don't let personal issues interfere. Needing accommodation is seen as a weakness.

13.2.2 The always-on mentality

Early morning calls with Asia. Late evening calls with Europe. Weekend emails. The expectation that you're available 24/7. This leaves no room for rest, recovery, or self-care—the very things your changing body desperately needs.

13.2.3 The youth-worship culture

In industries that prize innovation and disruption, there's often an implicit bias toward younger workers. Women in their 40s and 50s already face age discrimination. Adding "menopausal symptoms" to the mix feels like career suicide.

13.2.4 The performance metrics

Your worth is measured in deliverables, targets, and KPIs. There's no metric for "managing a hormonal transition while running a department." If your performance dips even slightly, there's someone younger, hungrier, and willing to work harder.

13.2.5 The lack of understanding

Most corporate policies around health focus on maternity leave, occasional sick days, or catastrophic illness. There's no framework for supporting someone through a multi-year hormonal transition that affects them daily but doesn't fit into traditional "sick" or "healthy" categories.

13.2.6 The gendered nature of the workplace

Let's be honest: most corporate environments were designed by men, for men. The temperature (too cold for many women, especially those having hot flashes), the meeting schedules (no consideration for energy fluctuations), the work hours (incompatible with disrupted sleep), even the office furniture—none of it was designed with women's hormonal health in mind.

All of this creates an environment where women feel they must hide their symptoms, push through exhaustion, and pretend everything is fine—even when it's very much not fine.

13.3 The Hidden Toll of Silence

When Sarah first started experiencing symptoms, she did what most high-achieving women do: she tried to power through.

Brain fog? She worked longer hours to compensate. Exhaustion? More coffee, more willpower. Memory issues? More detailed notes, more checklists. Hot flashes during presentations? She blamed the room temperature and kept going. Anxiety before big meetings? She told herself to "get it together."

She didn't tell her boss. She didn't tell her colleagues. She didn't even tell her work friends.

She suffered alone. And it nearly broke her.

Here's what happens when women try to manage perimenopausal symptoms in silence:

13.3.1 Physical toll:

- Chronic stress exacerbates symptoms
- Sleep deprivation compounds exhaustion
- No time for proper meals or exercise
- Health issues worsen without intervention

13.3.2 Mental toll:

- Constant anxiety about being "found out."
- Fear of losing credibility or opportunities
- Shame about not being able to "handle it."
- Isolation due to lack of support

13.3.3 Professional toll:

- Performance genuinely suffers from untreated symptoms
- Missed opportunities because of low energy or confidence

- Strained relationships with colleagues due to irritability or withdrawal
- Decisions made from a place of fear rather than strategy

The cruel irony: the silence itself makes everything worse.

13.4 What Your Body Actually Needs During the Workday

Let's talk about what's happening in your body during a typical high-stress work day during perimenopause:

Morning (6:00 AM - 9:00 AM):

You wake up exhausted because you were up at 3 AM with night sweats and racing thoughts. Your cortisol (stress hormone) spikes as you rush to get ready, check emails, and prepare for the day.

Your body needs: gentle movement, protein-rich breakfast, hydration, and a few minutes of calm before the chaos.

What actually happens: you skip breakfast, chug coffee, immediately dive into emails while getting ready, and start your day already depleted.

Mid-morning (9:00 AM - 12:00 PM):

You're in back-to-back meetings. Your blood sugar drops. Your focus wavers. A hot flash hits during your presentation. You push through.

Your body needs: a healthy snack, water, a brief movement break, and cool air.

What actually happens: more coffee, maybe a pastry from the meeting room, sitting still for hours, suffering through the hot flash silently.

Afternoon (12:00 PM - 3:00 PM):

Your energy crashes. Brain fog sets in. You have three more hours of high-stakes work ahead.

Your body needs: a nourishing lunch, a 20-minute rest or walk, and time away from screens.

What actually happens: you work through lunch or grab something quick at your desk, push through the fog with sheer willpower and more caffeine.

Late Afternoon/Evening (3:00 PM - 7:00 PM):

You're running on fumes. Your patience is thin. Everything feels harder than it should.

Your body needs: lighter work, completion of the day, transition time before home responsibilities.

What actually happens: some of your most demanding work happens now—deadline pressures, difficult conversations, problem-solving—when your resources are lowest.

Night (7:00 PM onwards):

You come home depleted. Your family needs you. You still have emails to answer. You fall into bed exhausted.

Your body needs: nourishing food, gentle movement, stress release, and an early bedtime.

What actually happens: you manage everyone else's needs, answer work messages, maybe have wine to "unwind," fall into bed late, and start the cycle again.

Day after day. Week after week. Month after month.

This is not sustainable. And it's not necessary.

13.5 The Five Pillars of Thriving at Work after 35

After working with dozens of corporate women and experiencing this myself as a business owner, I've identified five essential pillars for maintaining your health and your career during this transition:

PILLAR 1: Energy Management Over Time Management

You've probably mastered time management. You know how to schedule, prioritize, and delegate. That's not the issue.

The issue is energy.

After 35, your energy is no longer unlimited or predictable. Some days you have it. Some days you don't. And no amount of time management will create energy that isn't there.

The shift: start managing your energy strategically.

Map your energy patterns:

For two weeks, track your energy levels throughout the day:

- When do you feel most alert and focused?

- When does the afternoon crash hit?
- What activities drain you most?
- What activities energize you?
- How does your cycle affect your energy (if you're still menstruating)?

Then restructure your work around your energy:

Schedule your most demanding work during your peak energy times. If you're sharp in the morning, that's when you do strategic thinking, important presentations, and complex problem-solving.

Protect your low-energy times. If afternoons are hard, schedule less demanding tasks then—emails, administrative work, team check-ins.

Build in recovery time. High-energy output requires recovery. If you have an intense morning, protect your afternoon. If you have a high-stakes presentation, keep the rest of that day lighter.

Use your calendar strategically:

- Block "focus time" for deep work during your peak hours
- Schedule meetings during mid-energy times
- Leave buffer time between meetings (even 10 minutes makes a difference)
- Protect one day per week from meetings if possible
- Say no to early morning or late evening calls when you can

PILLAR 2: Strategic Stress Management

Stress during perimenopause isn't just unpleasant—it's physiologically different from stress at other life stages.

Here's why: **when estrogen declines, cortisol (your stress hormone) has more pronounced effects.** The stress that you could handle easily at 30 now hits harder at 40. It affects your sleep more. Your mood more. Your body composition is more.

You cannot eliminate work stress. But you can change how you respond to it.

Micro-practices throughout the day:

You don't need hour-long meditation sessions. You need moments of nervous system regulation scattered through your day.

Try these:

The 3-minute reset between meetings:

- Close your eyes
- Take 5 deep breaths (4 counts in, 6 counts out)
- Roll your shoulders
- Drink water
- This simple practice prevents stress accumulation

The bathroom breathing break: When you feel overwhelmed, excuse yourself to the bathroom:

- 2 minutes of slow, deep breathing
- Cool water on your wrists and face
- A moment of stillness

- Return calmer and clearer

The lunchtime walks: Even 10 minutes outside, walking, changes your physiology:

- Lowers cortisol
- Improves mood
- Clears brain fog
- Provides movement your body craves

The evening transition ritual: Create a boundary between work and home:

- 5-minute breathing practice in your car before going home
- Change your clothes to signal the shift
- Brief yoga stretches
- Helps you show up for your family from a grounded place

Reframe stress responses:

When you notice stress rising—heart racing, jaw clenching, breath shallow—instead of pushing through, pause and ask:

"What does my body need right now?"

Sometimes it's breath. Sometimes it's water. Sometimes it's movement. Sometimes it's stepping away from your desk for 3 minutes.

These tiny interventions prevent stress from becoming chronic, accumulated, and damaging.

PILLAR 3: Protecting Your Focus and Cognitive Function

Brain fog is one of the most distressing symptoms for high-achieving women. You're used to being sharp, articulate, and quick. And suddenly you're:

- Forgetting words mid-sentence
- Losing your train of thought
- Walking into rooms and forgetting why
- Reading emails three times and still not absorbing them
- Missing details you'd normally catch

This isn't early dementia. This is a hormonal fluctuation affecting your brain.

Estrogen influences neurotransmitters, blood flow to the brain, and neural connectivity. When it fluctuates wildly during perimenopause, cognitive function fluctuates too.

The good news: there are practical strategies that help.

Cognitive support strategies:

1. Prioritize sleep above everything

Brain fog is dramatically worse with poor sleep. Your #1 cognitive strategy is better sleep (we covered this in earlier chapters). Everything else is secondary.

2. Front-load your day

Do your most cognitively demanding work early, when your brain is freshest. By afternoon, your cognitive resources are depleted—plan accordingly.

3. Externalize your memory

Stop relying on your memory. Use systems:

- Detailed calendar with reminders
- Task management apps
- Voice memos for ideas
- Immediate note-taking in meetings
- Checklists for complex processes

This isn't a failure—it's a smart adaptation.

4. Single-task instead of multi-task

Your brain can't handle the cognitive load of multitasking the way it used to. Focus on one thing at a time. Close other tabs. Silence notifications. Give yourself the gift of singular focus.

5. Take real breaks

Your brain needs recovery time. Every 60-90 minutes:

- Stand up
- Move
- Look away from screens
- Let your mind wander briefly

6. Nourish your brain

Your brain needs:

- Adequate protein (neurotransmitter production)
- Omega-3 fatty acids (brain structure and function)
- B vitamins (cognitive function)
- Stable blood sugar (consistent glucose for brain energy)

Skipping meals or living on coffee crashes your cognitive function.

7. Manage the moment when words escape you

It will happen—your mid-presentation, and suddenly you can't find a word. Instead of panicking:

"The word I'm looking for isn't coming to me right now, but the concept is..." and explain it differently. Or pause, take a breath, and if it doesn't come, move on. Everyone forgets words sometimes—it's only a big deal if you make it one.

My experience:

I teach yoga classes and conduct therapy sessions—both require clear communication. When I'm tired or stressed, words escape me more. Instead of fighting it, I've learned to:

- Prepare more thoroughly for important sessions
- Have notes visible (even if I don't use them, they're backup)
- Give myself grace when words don't come
- Focus on the essence of what I'm communicating, not perfect articulation

The fog does lift. Symptoms fluctuate. On good days, your brain works beautifully. On hard days, you adapt.

PILLAR 4: Setting Boundaries (Without Guilt)

This is often the hardest shift for high-achieving women: **learning to say no.**

You're used to:

- Being available whenever needed
- Taking on extra projects

- Proving your worth through volume of work
- Putting others' needs before your own

During perimenopause, this pattern will destroy you.

Your body doesn't have the resources it used to. Your energy is finite. Your stress tolerance is lower. **You cannot keep operating at the same pace and expect to remain healthy.**

Boundaries aren't selfish. They're essential.

Practical boundaries for corporate women:

Time boundaries:

- No emails after 8 PM or before 8 AM (unless genuinely urgent)
- Lunch is non-negotiable—even 20 minutes
- One meeting-free day per week if possible
- No weekend work unless absolutely critical
- Protected time for personal health practices

Workload boundaries:

- Before accepting new projects, ask: "What will I stop doing to make room for this?"
- Delegate more-let go of needing to do everything yourself
- Say no to requests that don't align with your core responsibilities
- Be honest about capacity: "I don't have bandwidth for this right now."

Communication boundaries:

- You don't need to respond to every message immediately
- You don't need to justify taking time off

- You don't need to apologize for having limits
- You don't need to explain your health situation unless you choose to

Energy boundaries:

- Protect your peak performance hours
- Decline meetings during your low-energy times when possible
- Leave events early when you're depleted
- Choose which evening/social work events actually matter

The guilt will come. You'll feel like you're letting people down. Like you're not doing enough. Like you're being difficult.

But here's the truth: boundaries allow you to sustain your career long-term. Burnout doesn't.

PILLAR 5: Strategic Disclosure (When and How to Talk About It)

Should you tell your boss you're in perimenopause? Your colleagues? Your team?

There's no universal answer. It depends on:

- Your workplace culture
- Your relationship with your manager
- Your level of symptoms
- Legal protections in your location
- Your personal comfort level

Some women choose full openness. Some choose selective disclosure. Some choose to keep it private and manage symptoms through other strategies.

All of these choices are valid.

If you choose to disclose, here's how to do it strategically:

1. Frame it professionally, not apologetically

Instead of: "I'm sorry, I'm going through menopause, and I'm a mess."

Try: "I want to let you know I'm managing a hormonal transition that sometimes affects my sleep and energy. I'm working with healthcare providers to optimize my health, and I may occasionally need flexibility with meeting times or the option to work from home. My commitment to my work remains strong, and I'm implementing strategies to maintain my performance."

2. Focus on solutions, not just problems

"Here's what I'm experiencing, and here's what would help me continue performing well..."

3. Know your rights

In many countries, menopause-related symptoms are protected under disability discrimination or health accommodation laws. Research what protections exist in your location.

4. Choose your audience carefully

You might tell your direct manager, but not broadcast it widely. Or tell HR to explore accommodation options. Or confide in trusted colleagues who might be experiencing similar things.

5. Educate if you're comfortable

Sometimes people are ignorant, not malicious. Sharing information about what perimenopause actually is can create understanding and support.

If you choose NOT to disclose:

That's also completely valid. You can:

- Request accommodations without explaining why ("I work better with flexible hours" or "I need a fan in my office")
- Take sick days when symptoms are severe
- Manage symptoms through all the strategies in this book
- Build support outside of work

Your health information is yours to share or not share as you choose.

13.6 The Accommodation Conversation

If you decide to request accommodations, be specific:

Instead of: "I need help because I'm struggling."

Try:

- "I'd like to request flexible start times 2-3 days per week to accommodate some health appointments."
- "I'm requesting the option to work from home when needed to manage a medical condition."
- "I'd like to explore adjusting my meeting schedule to cluster them in the mornings when I'm most effective."
- "Could we install a fan or adjust the temperature in my workspace?"
- "I'd like to reduce travel requirements temporarily while I'm managing a health transition."

When women support each other through this transition, workplaces become more humane for everyone.

13.7 The Career Question: Stay or Go?

Some women reach a point where they wonder: "Should I just leave? Take a break? Downshif my career?"

There's no right answer. But here are questions to consider:

Are you wanting to leave because:

- Your symptoms are unmanaged and overwhelming? (Address the symptoms first)
- Your workplace is genuinely toxic and unsupportive? (Leaving might be wise)
- You're burned out from decades of high performance? (Maybe it's time for a change)

- You're experiencing a deeper life re-evaluation? (Common during this transition)

Or are you wanting to leave because:

- You're afraid of being "found out"? (Consider whether disclosure or symptom management might help)
- You assume you can't perform at the level you used to? (This often isn't true once symptoms are managed)
- You're internalizing ageist or sexist messages? (Your value doesn't diminish with age)

Many women who consider leaving during the worst of perimenopause find that once symptoms are managed, they rediscover their professional passion and capability.

But some genuinely are ready for a change—and that's also valid.

This transition often brings clarity about what truly matters. If your career no longer aligns with your values or desired lifestyle, **perimenopause might be the catalyst for a meaningful pivot.**

Just make sure you're making decisions from a place of empowerment, not desperation.

13.8 The Opportunity in This Transition

Here's something that often gets lost in discussions about perimenopause and work:

Many women report that they become better leaders during and after this transition.

Why?

Greater emotional intelligence: Navigating your own vulnerability builds empathy and understanding for others' struggles.

Clearer priorities: When energy is limited, you become ruthless about what truly matters. This clarity makes you more effective.

Stronger boundaries: Learning to say no and protect your wellbeing makes you a better role model for your team.

Deeper wisdom: Decades of experience combined with the self-knowledge that comes from this transition create powerful leadership.

More authenticity: Pretending becomes exhausting. Authenticity becomes easier—and more magnetic.

Less tolerance for nonsense: You have less patience for workplace politics, unnecessary drama, or inefficient processes. This directness can be refreshing and effective.

The women on the other side of this transition often report feeling more powerful, more confident, and more effective than ever before.

You're not losing your edge. You're gaining a different kind of edge.

13.9 A Letter to My Corporate Sisters

If you're reading this from your office at 9 PM, exhausted and wondering how much longer you can keep this up—

If you're sitting in your car in the parking lot, taking deep breaths before going into another day of pretending, you're fine—

If you're lying awake at 3 AM, anxious about a presentation tomorrow, knowing your brain won't be as sharp as you need it to be—

I see you. And I want you to know:

You are not failing. Your value hasn't diminished. Your capabilities haven't disappeared.

Your body is going through a profound biological transition, and you're trying to navigate it while maintaining a high-performance career in a system that was never designed to support you through this.

That's not a personal failure. **That's a systemic failure.**

But while we work to change systems—and we should—you also need strategies for today, tomorrow, next week.

You can thrive during this transition. Not by being superhuman. By being strategic:

Strategic about your energy. Strategic about your stress management. Strategic about protecting your cognitive function. Strategic about your boundaries. Strategic about when and how you ask for support.

You don't have to choose between your health and your career. But you do have to manage them both intentionally.

And on the days when you can't do it all perfectly—when the hot flash comes during the board meeting, when you forget a word during the presentation, when exhaustion wins, and you leave work early—

Give yourself the same grace you'd give a colleague going through a health challenge.

You are navigating something genuinely difficult. **And you're doing it while still showing up, still contributing, still leading.**

That's not a weakness. That's a strength.

Your career is a marathon, not a sprint. Pace yourself for longevity, not just immediate performance.

The women who will thrive in the decades ahead aren't the ones who pushed hardest through perimenopause at the expense of their health.

They're the ones who learned to work with their bodies, set boundaries, ask for support, and emerge from this transition with their health and their careers intact.

You can be one of them.

PART 6

YOUR 30-DAY TRANSFORMATION PLAN

CHAPTER 14

YOUR HORMONAL HARMONY TOOLKIT

Figure 11: Daily Tools for Hormonal Balance

The Essentials for Your 30-Day Reset

Before you begin your transformation, you need your toolkit. Think of this chapter as your reference guide. You don't need to master everything at once, but these are the "ingredients" we will use to cook up your 30-day plan.

After 35, our hormones are highly sensitive to **rhythm**. When we lack a routine, the body stays in a state of "high alert." By adopting a Yogic Dincharya (Daily Routine), you tell your nervous system: "You are safe. You are supported. You can find balance."

14.1 The Morning Momentum (Dincharya)

Your morning determines your hormonal health. Instead of reaching for your phone—which triggers an immediate hit of dopamine and cortisol—we follow the "Step-by-Step Awakening."

14.1.1 The First Hydration:

Before coffee or tea, drink 500 ml of warm water. This "wakes up" the digestive fire (**Agni**) and helps flush out toxins (**Ama**) accumulated overnight.

14.1.2 The Internal Observation:

Spend 2 minutes sitting on the edge of your bed. Check in: How is my energy? Where is my breath?

14.1.3 The Sun Salutation:

Even if you don't do a full workout, 5 minutes of stretching or a few rounds of sun salutation toward the light signals your brain to stop producing Melatonin (sleep hormone) and start producing Serotonin (mood stabilizer).

14.2 The Yoga Pharmacy (Asana)

For a woman over 35, yoga isn't about flexibility; it's about **endocrine health**. Here are a few "Golden Poses" we will use:

14.2.1 Bridge Pose (Setu Bandha Sarvangasana)

For pelvic support and gentle thyroid stimulation.

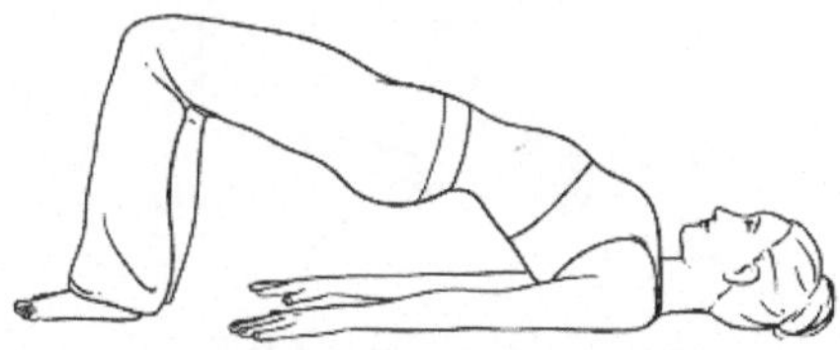

Figure 12: Bridge Pose (Setubandhasana)

Sthiti: Supine
Bend knees, feet hip-width apart. Lift hips upward, interlock fingers beneath back if comfortable. Keep your neck relaxed. Hold the pose for 5 breaths.

14.3.2 Cat-Cow Flow (Marjaryasana-Bitilasana):

To wake up the spine and stimulate the thyroid gland.

Figure 13: Cat-Cow Pose

Sthiti: Table Top

On hands and knees, inhale to arch your back (look up), exhale to round your spine (look at your navel). Repeat for 5 -7 rounds.

14.2.3 Child's Pose (Balasana):

For adrenal fatigue. It turns the senses inward and quiets the "fight or flight" response.

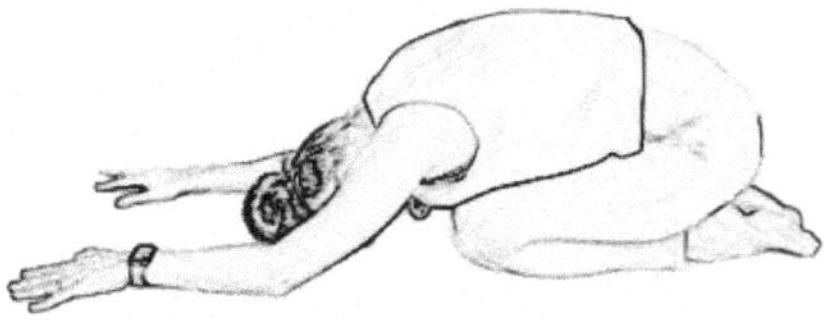

Figure 14: Child Pose

Sthiti: Thunderbolt Pose (Vajrasana)

Kneel, sit on your heels, and fold forward until your forehead rests on the mat or a pillow. Hold the pose for 5 - 7 breaths.

14.2.4 Half Spinal Twist (Ardha Matsyendrasana – gentle)

For digestion, spine mobility, and to regulate the adrenal glands.

Figure 15: Half Spinal Twist

Sthiti: Seated Position

Bend one knee, place the opposite elbow outside the thigh, and rotate gently from the spine. Keep shoulders relaxed. Hold the pose for 5 breaths and repeat on the other side.

14.2.5 Butterfly Pose (Baddha Konasana):

For pelvic circulation and hormonal balance.

Figure 16: Butterfly Pose

Sthiti: Seated Position

Sit with legs extended forward. Bend the knees and bring the soles of the feet together. Hold the feet with both hands and gently move the knees up and down like butterfly wings. Keep the spine tall and chest open. Repeat for 10 rounds.

14.2.6 Legs-up-the-Wall (Viparita Karani):

The ultimate hormone balancer. It drains the lymphatic system and lowers blood pressure.

Figure 17: Legs up the Wall (Viparita Karani)

Sthiti: Supine Position

Lie on your back with your legs resting vertically against a wall. Keep your hips on the floor or a small cushion. Stay in the position for up to 10 minutes.

14.2.7 Pigeon Pose (Supported Eka Pada Rajakapotasana)

For deep hip release and more circulation to the pelvic floor.

Figure 18: Pigeon Pose

Sthiti: Tabletop

Bring one knee forward, extend the opposite leg back. Use a cushion under the hips if needed. Keep your chest lifted. Hold the pose for 5 breaths and repeat on the other side

14.2.8 Plank Pose (Phalakasana)

For core strength and metabolic support.

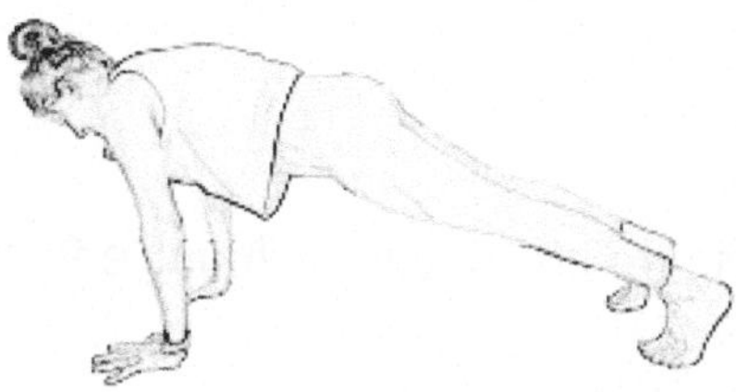

Figure 19: Plank Pose (Phalakasana)

Sthiti: Tabletop
Step both legs back, align shoulders over wrists, and keep body in one straight line. Engage your abdomen and breathe steadily. Hold the pose for 5 breaths.

14.2.9 Revolved Triangle (Parivrtta Trikonasana – gentle variation)

For balance and digestive stimulation.

Figure 20: Revolved Triangle Pose

Sthiti: Wide stance

Place one hand near the opp foot or block, rotate torso toward the front leg, and extend the opposite arm upward. Keep legs steady. Hold the pose for 5 breaths and repeat on the other side.

14.2.10 Triangle Pose (Trikonasana):

For stability and pelvic circulation.

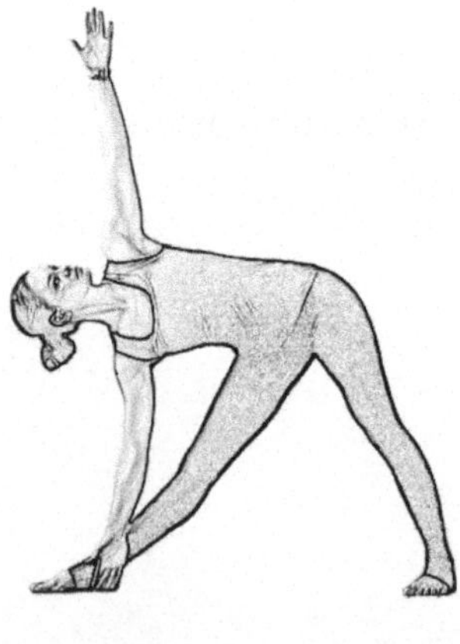

Figure 21: Triangle Pose

Sthiti: Tadasana

Stand wide. Reach one hand to your shin and the other to the sky. Keep your chest open and legs strong. Hold the pose for 5 breaths.

14.2.11 Corpse Pose (Shavasana):

Critical for integration. This is where the hormonal "reset" actually happens.

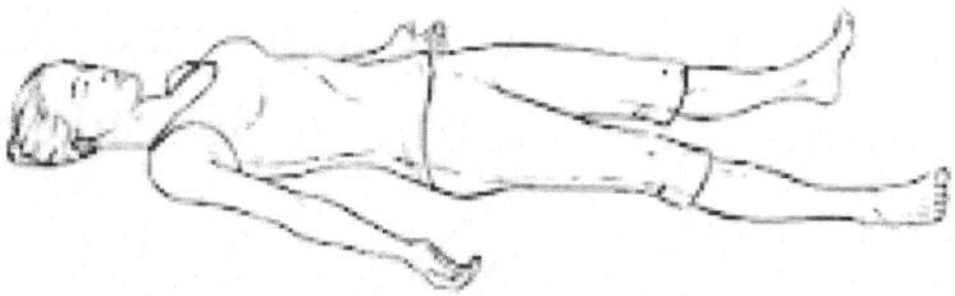

Figure 22: Corpse Pose (Shavasana)

Sthiti: Supine Position

Lie flat on your back, palms up, eyes closed. Relax every muscle and remain completely still

14.2.12 Warrior II (Virabhadrasana II)

For strength, grounding, and pelvic circulation

Figure 23: Warrior II Pose (Virabhadrasana II)

Sthiti: Wide standing stance
Turn one foot outward, bend the front knee, and extend arms parallel to the floor. Gaze over the front hand. Keep spine tall and shoulders relaxed. Hold the pose for 5 breaths and repeat on the other side.

14.3 The Breath Reset (Pranayama)

The breath is the only part of our autonomic nervous system we can consciously control.

14.3.1 Cleansing Breath (Kapalabhati – gentle)

Gentle, rhythmic exhalations with passive inhalation that help clear mental fog, support digestion, and energize the system. Best practiced in the morning, not before sleep.

Figure 24: Cleansing Breath (Kapalbhati)

Sit in a meditative posture, exhale forcefully by contracting the abdominal muscles, and allow passive inhalation. Keep the spine erect and avoid body movements.

Avoid if you have high blood pressure, heart issues, or severe respiratory conditions.

14.3.2 Sectional Breathing (Vibhagiya Pranayama)- Abdominal, Chest, Clavicular, Full Yogic Breathing

Increases lung capacity, improves oxygen intake, and enhances awareness of breathing. No limitations.

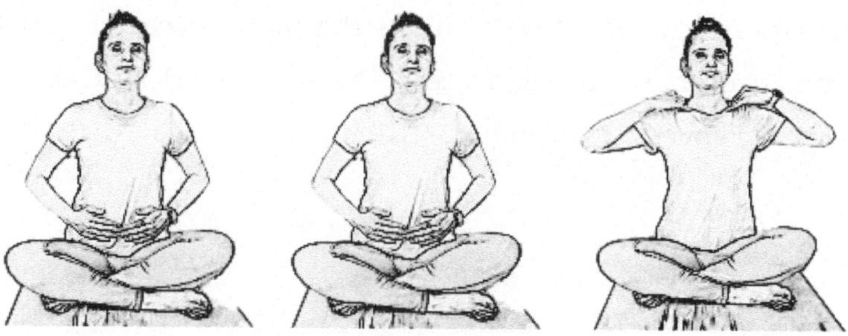

Figure 25: Sectional Breathing (Vibhagiya Pranayama)

Breathe deeply in three stages: expand the abdomen, then the chest, and lift the collarbones. Exhale first from the collarbones, chest, and then the abdomen. Repeat for 5 rounds in each section.

14.3.3 Victorious Breath(Ujjayi Pranayama)

Calms the nervous system, regulates body temperature, and enhances mental clarity. Avoid if you have high blood pressure, heart conditions, or throat issues.

Figure 26: Victorious Breath (Ujjayi Pranayama)

14.3.4 Nerve Cleansing Breath (Nadi Shodhana):

Alternate nostril breathing. This is the most powerful tool for a woman over 35 to balance the "Solar" (active) and "Lunar" (receptive) energies within her.

Figure 27: Alternate Nostril Breathing (Nadi Shodhana)

Sit in a meditative posture, inhale through one nostril, exhale through the other, alternating sides using Nasika Mudra. Repeat for 9 rounds.

14.3.5 Left-Nostril Breathing (Chandra Bhedana)

Breathing through the left nostril to activate calming, cooling energy. Helps reduce anxiety, irritability, and emotional overwhelm—especially supportive for women over 35. Avoid if you have a cold, low blood pressure, or depression

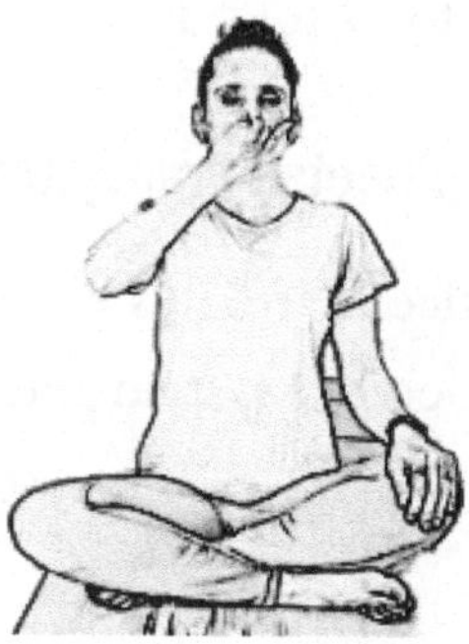

Figure 28: Left Nostril Breathing (Chandra Bhedana)

Sit in a meditative posture. Inhale through the left nostril, exhale through the right using Nasika Mudra. Repeat for 9 rounds

14.3.6 Right-Nostril Breathing (Surya Bhedana)

Breathing through the right nostril to stimulate warming and activate energy. Improves alertness and motivation; best avoided late in the evening

Figure 29: Right Nostril Breathing (Surya Bhedana)

Inhale through the right nostril and exhale through the left using Nasika Mudra. Repeat for 9 rounds.

14.3.7 Cooling Breath (Sheetali Pranayama)

A cooling breath practice that helps reduce the intensity of hot flashes by calming the nervous system and lowering internal body heat.

Figure 30: Cooling Breath (Sheetali Pranayama)

Curl your tongue into a tube shape, inhale deeply through the mouth, and exhale through the nose. Repeat for 9 rounds. Avoid in cold weather or if you have asthma or low blood pressure.

14.4. The Sattvic Kitchen (Dietary Anchors)

We don't do "diets" here; we do **nourishment**.

14.4.1 The Three-Hour Rule:

Try to finish your last meal at least three hours before bed to allow your hormones to focus on "repair" rather than "digestion" while you sleep.

14.4.2 Hormone-Loving Fats:

Including Ghee, avocado, or walnuts in your meals to provide the raw materials your body needs to manufacture estrogen and progesterone.

14.4.3 The Protein Anchor:

Ensure every breakfast contains protein to prevent the mid-morning sugar crash that leads to irritability.

14.5 The Evening Wind-Down

To have a successful Dincharya tomorrow, you must start tonight.

14.5.1 The Brain Dump:

Writing down three things you are grateful for and three things on your to-do list to "empty" the mind before sleep.

14.5.2 The Dimming:

Reducing artificial light to allow your natural sleep cycles to take over.

14.5.3 Physical practice:

You may add gentle stretches or restorative poses.

14.5.4 The Belly Breath:

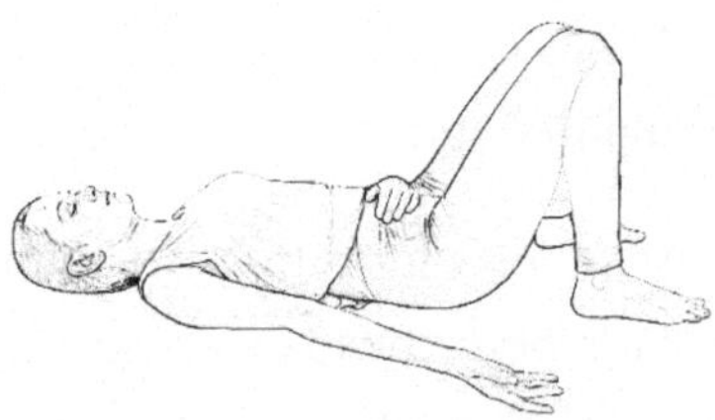

Figure 31: Belly Breath

Slow, diaphragmatic breathing that calms the mind, reduces stress, and helps the body unwind before sleep. Place one hand gently on the abdomen and feel it rise softly as you inhale and fall naturally as you exhale, allowing the breath to deepen and relax the body.

14.5.5 Humming Bee Breath (Bhramari Pranayama):

The soothing vibration stimulates the vagus nerve, calming the nervous system, easing evening anxiety, and preparing the body for restful sleep.

Figure 32: Humming Bee Breath (Bhramari Pranayama)

14.5.6 Emotional Grounding

Supporting mood and inner steadiness

Hormonal changes often increase emotional sensitivity.

Support the emotional body with:

- Yoga Nidra
- Om Meditation

14.5.6.1 Yoga Nidra – Conscious Deep Rest

After 35, many women live primarily in their heads — thinking, planning, managing, and processing emotions. This mental overactivity disturbs pranic balance and affects sleep and hormonal stability. Yoga Nidra is an ancient practice described in the Upanishads, particularly the Mandukya Upanishad. Of the four states of consciousness — waking, dreaming, deep sleep, and turiya — Yoga Nidra refers to conscious awareness of deep sleep (prajna), symbolized by the "M" of AUM. It is not ordinary sleep, but a subtle state beyond the fluctuations of the waking and dreaming mind.

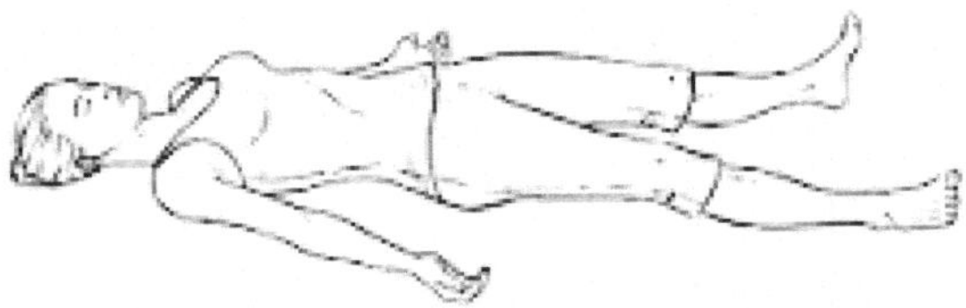

Lie in Shavasana with the head, neck, and spine aligned. Rest on a firm yet comfortable surface. Allow the breath to become smooth and effortless.

Gently rotate awareness through the body — from the head and face to the throat, shoulders, arms, hands, chest, abdomen, hips, legs, and feet. Do not move the body; only move attention. Then reverse the journey, moving from the toes back up to the head. Feel as though the breath flows through each region as awareness passes. This systematic rotation of consciousness deeply relaxes the nervous system and balances pranic flow.

If practicing more deeply, guide awareness along the spinal axis — exhaling from the crown to the base of the spine, inhaling from the base to the crown. Allow attention to rest gently at the eyebrow center, throat, and finally the heart space. In the heart region, let awareness dissolve into stillness.

Remain in that silence without effort. When thoughts return, gently bring awareness back to the breath and physical body. Slowly move the fingers and toes, and open the eyes — carrying the stillness with you.

Yoga Nidra may be practiced for a few minutes for deep relaxation or for longer periods as preparation for meditation. It is a powerful tool for restoring nervous system balance, improving sleep quality, and cultivating inner stability.

14.5.6.2 OM Meditation – Returning to Inner Balance

Beyond the age of 35, a woman's life often becomes fuller and more demanding. Hormonal shifts, emotional responsibilities, and constant mental engagement can leave the nervous system overstimulated. OM meditation offers a gentle yet profound way to restore inner balance and deep rest.

Begin by preparing the breath with a few rounds of Kapalabhati, sectional breathing, Nadi Shuddhi, and Bhramari, allowing awareness to move from audible vibration (Ahata) to inner resonance (Anahata). Sit comfortably with the spine erect and the body relaxed.

Start by chanting OM aloud with the eyes open, feeling the vibration in the chest and throat. After a few rounds, close your eyes and gradually allow the chanting to become mental. Repeat OM silently in a smooth, continuous flow. If thoughts arise, slightly increase the speed of repetition so the mind has no space to wander. Once steadiness returns, allow the chanting to slow naturally. If distractions reappear, gently adjust the speed again. This creates an unbroken stream of awareness.

As the chanting becomes softer and more effortless, begin to feel its subtle vibration within the body. Gradually, this vibration spreads throughout. With further slowing, you will notice the quiet gap between two OMs. Allow that space to widen without effort, dissolving into silence. Rest in this silence. Awareness expands beyond the body into a spacious presence. This effortless state, known as Ajapa, becomes a source of clarity, creativity, strength, and inner bliss.

From this deep stillness in the heart region, let one OM arise softly as an audible sound, allowing its vibration to spread through the entire body and the space around you. Gently blink the eyes open and return with awareness.

Even a few moments of this practice during the day can calm the sympathetic nervous system, regulate stress hormones, support healthy blood pressure, and steady emotional fluctuations. More than a technique, OM meditation becomes a quiet anchor — restoring balance from within.

A Gentle Reminder

Hormonal harmony doesn't come from doing more.
It comes from **showing up consistently with care**.

In the next chapter, you'll be guided step by step through a **30-day hormonal reset**, where these tools come together in a clear, realistic structure — so you don't have to figure it out on your own.

CHAPTER 15

THE 30-DAY HORMONAL RESET

A gentle, structured way to restore rhythm, strength, and balance

15.1 Before You Begin (Please Read)

This 30-day reset is designed to be supportive, not demanding.

If you have a medical condition, are recovering from surgery, or are under medical care, please consult your doctor before beginning any new wellness routine and practice under the supervision of a certified yoga therapist.
Listen to your body.
This is a guide — not a prescription.

15.2 How to Use This 30-Day Reset

This reset is built on **rhythm**, not intensity.
Some elements stay the same every day to calm your nervous system.
Others change weekly to support your body's natural progression.

What stays the same every day:

- Morning Momentum (Dincharya)
- Evening Wind-Down
- Dietary anchors

What changes week by week:

- Morning yoga theme
- Morning pranayama focus

You will practice **6 days a week**, with **Sunday as a free-movement day**.

Sunday: Your Free-Movement Day

Sunday is not about "doing nothing."
It's about **moving in a way that feels joyful and natural**.

Choose what you genuinely enjoy:

- Walking in nature
- Swimming
- Light sports
- Dancing
- Gentle stretching with music
- Any movement that feels nourishing, not exhausting

Gentle reminder:

Joyful movement supports hormones just as much as structured practice.

You will continue your **evening wind-down** on Sundays.

15.3 WEEK 1 — Stabilize & Ground

Purpose:

Calm the nervous system, improve sleep, and create a sense of safety in the body.

This week sets the foundation for everything that follows.

Week 1 Practice Overview

Element	Practice
Morning Yoga (20 mins)	Cat–Cow Gentle spinal rotations Sun Salutation (1-3 rounds) Forward fold Child Pose Legs-Up-the-Wall Shavasana
Morning Pranayama (10 mins)	Cleansing Breath Belly Breathing Intercostal Breathing Clavicle Breathing Full Yogic Breathing
Evening Wind down (5 mins)	Abdominal Breathing Full yogic breathing Humming Bee Breathing (Bhramari)
Meditation (15-20 mins)	Fri / Sat – OM chanting
Sunday	Free-movement day

Table 1: Week 1 Practice

What this week supports

- Better sleep quality
- Reduced anxiety and restlessness
- Improved stress tolerance

Gentle self-check

By the end of this week, notice:

- Are you falling asleep more easily?
- Does your body feel less tense?
- Is your breathing naturally slower?

Reflection prompt

What does "slowing down" feel like in my body?

15.4 WEEK 2 — Build & Energize

Purpose:

Support strength, metabolism, circulation, and confidence.

Once the nervous system is calmer, the body is ready to build.

Week 2 Practice Overview

Element	Practice
Morning Yoga (20 mins)	• Sun Salutation (you may increase the number of rounds from the first week) • Butterfly • Chair Pose • Warrior • Plank • Bridge Pose • Supine twist • Shavasana
Morning Pranayama (10 mins)	Cleansing Breath Full Yogic Breathing Victorious Breath (Ujjayi) Alternate Nostril Breathing
Evening Wind down (5 mins)	Abdominal Breathing (inhale: exhale; 2:4) Humming Bee Breathing
Meditation (15-20 mins)	Fri / Sat - Yoga Nidra
Sunday	Free-movement day

Table 2: Week 2 Practice

What this week supports

- Stable energy levels
- Improved metabolism
- Increased confidence and resilience

Gentle self-check

Notice:

- Do you feel stronger or more stable?
- Is your energy more consistent during the day?

Reflection prompt

What kind of strength does my body need right now?

15.5 WEEK 3 — Release & Restore

Purpose:

Support digestion, circulation, detoxification, and emotional release. This week helps the body let go of accumulated tension.

Week 3 Practice Overview

Element	Practice
Morning Yoga (20 mins)	• Revolved wide-legged Forward Bend • Revolved Triangle pose • Seated spinal twist • Butterfly pose • Pigeon pose • Cobra Twist • Crossed Leg lumbar stretch • Shavasana

Morning Pranayama (10 mins)	Cleansing Breath Full Yogic Breathing Victorious Breath (Ujjayi) Alternate Nostril Breathing (inhale: exhale 2:4 or 3:6)
Evening Wind down (5 mins)	Abdominal Breathing Left Nostril Breathing Humming Bee Breathing (Bhramari)
Meditation (15-20 mins)	Fri / Sat Yoga Nidra/Guided Relaxation
Sunday	Free-movement day

Table 3: Week 3 Practice

What this week supports

- Improved digestion
- Reduced bloating and heaviness
- Emotional lightness and clarity

Gentle self-check

Notice:

- Does your body feel lighter?
- Are emotions moving more freely?

Reflection prompt

What am I ready to release — physically or emotionally?

WEEK 4 — Listen & Choose

This week is about **self-trust**.
By now, you've experienced how different practices affect you.
Choose your morning yoga and pranayama based on how you feel:

How You Are Feeling	Choose This Practice Focus
Feeling anxious	**Stabilise & Ground (Week 1)**
Feeling dull or heavy	**Build & Energise (Week 2)**
Feeling bloated or stuck	**Release & Renew (Week 3)**
Feeling exhausted	**Restorative Poses, Cooling Breathing Practices & Meditation**

Table 4: Week 4 practice

Your evening wind-down remains the same.

A Final Gentle Reminder

Hormonal harmony doesn't come from perfection.
It comes from rhythm, awareness, and kindness toward your body.

This 30-day reset is not the end — it's the beginning of a more intuitive way of living.

Resources:

1. Harvard Business Review. (2020). *Focus on "Microhabits" to Change Your Behavior.* Retrieved from https://hbr.org/tip/2020/03/focus-on-microhabits-to-change-your-behavior
2. Benson, H., et al. (2013). Relaxation response induces temporal transcriptome changes. *PLoS ONE.*
3. Jerath, R., et al. (2006). Physiology of long pranayamic breathing. *Medical Hypotheses.*
4. Patañjali. *Yoga Sūtras*, Chapter 1, Verse 1.14.
5. Nooraini Aliyas, Dr. Satyam Tripathi, and Dr. Amit Singh. *Therapeutic Guidelines of Yoga Therapy & Integrative Medicine.* Swami Paramahansa Samsthana, 2021.
6. Praśna Upaniṣad, Chapter 2, Mantra 13.
7. Mandukya Upanishad with Gaudapada Karika, Chapter 3, Verse 44.
8. World Health Organization, Food and Agriculture Organization of the United Nations, & United Nations University. (2007). *Protein and amino acid requirements in human nutrition: Report of a joint WHO/FAO/UNU expert consultation* (WHO Technical Report Series No. 935). World Health Organization. https://iris.who.int/handle/10665/43411

ABOUT THE AUTHOR

Nidhi Kagrana is an Indian-origin, Singapore-based yoga therapist and founder of Balance2Bliss. Through her work, she supports women in understanding and navigating midlife hormonal transitions by integrating traditional yogic principles with contemporary scientific insight.

She is the creator of the course *Managing Menopause Naturally*, developed to offer structured, sustainable guidance for women seeking natural support. Her areas of focus include hormonal balance, nervous system regulation, and cultivating resilient daily rhythms for long-term health.

If you'd like to connect or explore her work further:
contact@balance2bliss.com

www.balance2bliss.com

सर्वे भवन्तु सुखिनः
सर्वे सन्तु निरामयाः ।
सर्वे भद्राणि पश्यन्तु
मा कश्चित् दुःखभाग्भवेत्
ॐ शान्तिः शान्तिः शान्तिः ॥

Sarve bhavantu sukhinaḥ
Sarve santu nirāmayāḥ |
Sarve bhadrāṇi paśyantu
Mā kaścid duḥkha-bhāg bhavet

Om Śāntiḥ Śāntiḥ Śāntiḥ||

May all beings be happy.
May all be free from illness.
May all see what is auspicious and uplifting.
May none suffer or be in sorrow.

Om Peace Peace Peace

— *Bṛhadāraṇyaka Upaniṣad 1.4.14*